OPEN
for Business

How to Achieve Professional Success
Using the Power of Chakras

Dear Carol,

I am so grateful
for you in my life!
May your chakras align!

Nanette

Nanette Giacoma, MBA, MA

Giacoma, Nanette
    Open for Business: How to Achieve Professional Success Using the
    Power of Chakras

ISBN: 978-1-7329169-0-6
Library of Congress Control Number 2018912889

Edited by Carol Chesney Hess, www.CarolChesneyHess.com
Cover illustration and design by Lisa Greenleaf
Interior layout, design, illustrations, and formatting by Lisa Greenleaf,
www.Lisagreenleaf.com

Dedication

To my husband and daughter for sharing their love, light, and energy with me. To my mom and dad for their eternal support in all that I do. And to all the amazing women in my life who encourage me every day to shine my light.

❧ Reviews ❧

Nanette Giacoma has written a very accessible, practical, and original book, combining two unlikely bedfellows – entrepreneurship and esoteric Eastern chakra theory. A plethora of fresh insights arise through this creative cross-fertilization. Drawing upon the ancient wisdom of the Hindu chakra model of the energy body, she utilizes this time-honored spiritual system, pertaining to the health and wholeness of the thriving human being, as a trustworthy guide for understanding what is necessary to generate health and wholeness in a thriving business.

The book contains an array of practical insights and a wealth of exercises for the entrepreneur aspiring for success, with many tools for diagnosing and correcting a business not yet attaining its full potential.

After outlining the essential issues represented by each chakra, she applies this perspective to similar issues that may arise for a business, a valid approach since both human being and business are living organisms. The heartfelt tone of the book is warm and encouraging, while not side-stepping difficult challenges. Nanette envisions and advocates for a flourishing business –one that pursues the highest good for all, a most refreshing clarion call in today's world.

Karen Jaenke, PhD
Chair, Consciousness & Transformative Studies
John F. Kennedy University
www.jfku.edu

Open for Business is a fresh perspective that offers real tools to tap into your inner source. This book is chock full of helpful tools that will help you get unstuck, and move you into an expansive mindset. I especially appreciated the Overcoming *Obstacles Exercise* in Chapter 5 for the third chakra.

It is easy to compartmentalize running a business and working in a professional field based in the spiritual, like my yoga studio. I found the wisdom for healing, not only for the imbalances in my business, but also (of course!) to heal the imbalances in myself.

It is a rare treat to have practical support while on our metaphysical business journeys. This book helps us to remember where it all begins, and how to truly be open for business. Thank you Nanette for embodying this in a graceful and balanced way.

Jennifer Nadeau, Owner
Jai Yoga
www.jaiyogahome.com

(continues on page 233)

ᗡᔡᔢ *Table of Contents* ᕼᔢᔡᗡ

❧ *Acknowledgments* ❧

My deepest gratitude to the many teachers and guides I have had the good fortune to encounter on my journey, as well as to my clients, who are always a source of inspiration and learning for me. A special thanks to my editor, Carol Hess (http://carolchesneyhess.com), who is the perfect blend of heart, soul, and no-nonsense to support me on my writing path.

ᘒᕷᘖ Introduction ᘒᕷᘖ

*Transformation literally means going
beyond your form.*
Wayne Dyer

ᕷᘖ

*We delight in the beauty of the butterfly, but rarely
admit the changes it has gone through to
achieve that beauty.*
Maya Angelou

I Want What She's Got!

Do you ever look at other leaders or other entrepreneurs like yourself and marvel at how they are thriving? They are manifesting their goals and then some. They are obviously on their way to exactly where they want to go, and – best of all – they are loving what they do. What have they got that you don't? Do you get the feeling that, whether you are climbing the corporate ladder or are the CEO of your own creative enterprise, something is missing? What are you missing? Why is business success eluding you?

You've probably been looking for what's missing, but no matter how many degrees you've acquired, trainings you've gone to, books you've read, workshops you've attended, or coaches you've hired, no one's been able to help you get what you need to achieve the level of accomplishment you crave. And no matter how many hours, days, weeks, months, and years you've spent in pursuit of becoming a master in your professional field, you probably don't know about the one crucial factor necessary to achieve true business success.

I understand because I've been where you are. For years and years and years, I searched for the secret formula to success. I did all the things I thought I was supposed to do to succeed. But I still felt like I was missing my mark. At one particularly low point, I even feared I had taken a wrong turn on my professional path. What started out feeling like a professional calling was beginning to feel like a professional fantasy. So I reached out to my spirit guides and asked for a sign that I was indeed on the right path. What I received in reply was a revelation! It was so simple, and yet so profound!

Still, I needed to convince my inner doubter of the validity of my revelation. In order to do this, I used it not only in my business, but with my clients as well. And sure enough, this was the answer my clients and I had been seeking. It truly helped us realize the personal and professional success we had previously been looking for to no avail.

Let me tell you a little about me and my story, and then I promise to share my revelation. It's going to make all the difference in the world to you. What's amazing is that it's a powerful system for creating both personal success in your life *and* professional success in your business or career. There's just one hitch. You've got to be willing to change – and to transform.

Transformational Change

If you are reading this book, then most certainly you are looking to change and transform something in your business. But there is a difference between change and transformation. What is it?

Every living being on the planet experiences change, but not every living being experiences transformation. Change happens when the seasons shift from winter to spring to summer to fall. Whether you live in a climate where the shifts are subtle or, like me, you live in a very changeable climate like New England, the truth is you probably are affected by your changing weather, but you are not likely to be transformed by it.

Seasonal changes happen personally and professionally as well, but these are the changes that have the potential to transform you. When you experience a personal or professional storm, how do you respond? Do you fight the change? Do you hunker down and hope it passes? Do you try to learn from it? Do you recognize it as a chance for transformation?

Transformation means you take the inevitable changes and use them to assist you in changing from a caterpillar into a butterfly – to go beyond your current form into infinite possibilities. The butterfly is a well-known symbol of transformation. Instinctively, the caterpillar knows it needs to go inside and have time to itself to do the hard work of becoming something beyond its present form. In the privacy of the chrysalis, the mysterious metamorphosis occurs.

Most likely a caterpillar has no idea it can be a butterfly, nor does it consciously make the changes to become one. And therein lies the difference between you and me and the caterpillar/butterfly. As humans, we frequently have to make a conscious effort to go from crawling to flying.

My Story: Transformation from a Master of Business Administration to a Master of Butterfly Awakening

Like a butterfly, I have crawled, and I have flown – and I have even done some dying. Because that's what transformational change demands. Change and transformation have been and continue to be present in my life. My business path has played a huge part in my transformation and soul growth. I'm hardly recognizable as the young MBA graduate of many years ago. Like the monarch caterpillar, I have metamorphosed into a butterfly and migrated thousands of miles to metaphorically die and be reborn again – caterpillar into butterfly – over and over.

I started as a retail manager at age twenty-three while at the same time pursuing my MBA. Shortly after receiving my degree, I switched into healthcare because I wanted to make a more meaningful difference in people's lives. Somewhere in the translation, "meaning" got lost, and I spent seven years pursuing the next rung in the corporate ladder. During that time, I frequently hid away parts of myself in order to be "successful." In retrospect, I realize some of my best gifts went underground in the pursuit of becoming who I thought I should be.

By age thirty-two, I was successfully climbing the corporate ladder, yet I felt a hole in my soul that couldn't be filled with money, power, or relationships. It wasn't long before I felt empty and depressed. In an effort to fill that hole, I began some deep soul searching – and that is where my conscious change and transformation began.

My search ultimately took me to earning a second master's degree – this time in art and consciousness studies, a funky blend of creativity, psychology, and spirituality that was a good fit for me. It was there that I was introduced to spirit guides, energy, and alternative ways of healing, doing, thinking, and being.

Thus began my double life – business administrator by day, a butterfly awakened by night. Somewhere in the back of my soul, I knew the two weren't separate, but for many years I didn't know how to bring them together in my professional career in a conscious way. I now see that in spite of myself, I used my awakened butterfly every day to transform myself, my life, and my business, and to support other team members on their path as well.

Then there came a time in my late thirties when I was ready to die a little and be reborn as a creativity business coach. I bumped along on this path for several years, with one foot in strategic planning and the other foot in creativity in business. While creativity in business is fairly common now, it was considered a little weird at the time. When offering my services to business leaders, I often got strange looks and the canned reply, "We don't have the funds for that right now."

I didn't dare talk to them about my real passion – holistic business practices based upon energy and spirituality. Now that is *really* weird! Despite my reluctance to reveal myself fully, my spirit guides had other plans. Synchronistic business opportunities, relationships, and education kept popping up to help me stay on track with my holistic business coaching desires.

Then tragedy hit. My younger brother by eight years died of alcoholism. It wasn't a complete surprise, but his death forced me into a chrysalis of mourning and reflection. During this time, I felt deeply moved to do some energy work. I knew my wounding was energetically lodged in my body and life. I sought to clear the energetic blocks to find more peace and clarity. I wanted to heal my sorrow and the associated parts of my family history.

I had thought about working with Reiki before but had never made the time to pursue it. In my chrysalis, I made the time. Over the next couple of years, I became a Usui Reiki Master and a Kundalini Reiki Master.

This led me deeper into energy work. I read many, many books and took online and in-person classes on Reiki, energy healing, chakras, quantum physics, the law of attraction, and other energy topics. I started to fully appreciate how energy influenced me physically and also how it moved within my life and business in both productive and nonproductive ways.

During this time, I also took an intensive yearlong Master Intuitive Coaching program with Colette Baron-Reid. Not only did I learn how to work with clients to help them do the deeply personal and spiritual work to make lasting shifts, but I was required to do my own transformational work.

Finally, it was time for me to come out of my chrysalis. I began teaching a Journey Circle workshop and incorporating alternative methods more intentionally with my clients. Once again, I deeply felt I had been called to this path. I was transformed. I had butterfly wings. I had metamorphosed into a holistic executive coach.

These days, I unabashedly talk about holistic ways of doing business – including energy and spirituality. Yes, some people think I'm totally weird. I've been called woo-woo (and worse). But it's practical woo-woo that works!

Then a couple of years ago, my spirit guides let me know there was more to be done. They called upon me to serve even more people. A book! Yes, it was time for me to write a book, they informed me. And suddenly I was back to being a caterpillar.

At first, I ignored their suggestion and instead spent time spinning my wheels on side projects. I rationalized my resistance by being super busy. I had a topic and an outline based on a class I had created earlier. Still, I procrastinated. After all, maybe there was a better topic.

And so I spun my wheels again by starting several other books but never completing any. Along the way, my guides kept giving me nudges that I already had *the topic*. My spirit guides had a tough job keeping me on my path, but they were very patient. They knew I was in the process of becoming a butterfly, and there is always enough time for soul growth. Finally, despite my fears and resistance, I ultimately listened to my guides and wrote this book.

I am spreading my butterfly wings once again! *Open for Business* is the culmination of over twenty-five years of walking between the worlds of traditional business and alternative methodologies. Throughout, I symbolically crawled into and flew out of my chrysalis as I transformed my knowledge and skills in traditional business to integrate them with alternative methods. My ultimate passion and desire is to create a system that will help leaders find their own set of butterfly wings that will fly them to a more holistic way of doing business. .

All Is Revealed

So you may be wondering, what's the profound revelation I received, and how will it help you succeed? It is quite simply this: When you apply the ancient chakra energy system and its principles to your business or your career, you will achieve professional success. And I'm going to tell you how to go about doing exactly that.

This book is unique because it's going to help you dig deep into your issues and challenges in a way you haven't done before. You will find answers to things you didn't even know you needed to ask, as well as solutions to problems and obstacles that have been tormenting you for ages. The processes in this book will enrich you and your business in ways you probably can't even imagine right now.

How to Use This Book

In addition to introductory and summary chapters, the book is structured in such a way that each chakra has its own chapter. While the information in this book builds upon the previous chapters to some degree, you may be drawn to work with a specific chakra before you work with those that precede it. I encourage you to follow your intuition where it leads you.

Each chakra chapter contains the following:

- *Chakra Quick Reference Guide*
- *Mandala Exercise*
- *Chakra Assessment* (downloadable as a PDF at www.nanettegiacoma.com/OpenForBusinessBook)
- *Guided Journey* (downloadable as an audio file at www.nanettegiacoma.com/OpenForBusinessBook))
- *Taking Action*
- *Ways to Balance Your Chakra*
- *Putting It Into Practice* (a case study of a business)
- *Notes* (downloadable as a PDF at www.nanettegiacoma.com/OpenForBusinessBook)

Also included in the book as appendixes are the *Business Chakra Solutions Guide* and *Goals Tracking Form* (downloadable as a PDF at www.nanettegiacoma.com/OpenForBusinessBook) *The Business Chakra Solutions Guide* can be used at any time – before, during, or after you read this book. It cross-references the most prevalent business issues with their corresponding chakras and indicates the chapters where you will find more information. This reference chart has been designed to help you focus your energy on your most pressing matters.

My intention is to give you multiple ways of working with your chakras so you can gain a more holistic picture of yourself and your business. Some of the processes may appeal to you more than others. In the spirit of transformation, I encourage you to not only do the processes that feel comfortable but also do those that feel uncomfortable. Transformation often requires that you try new and unfamiliar things.

While new processes can feel distressing at times, think of them as opportunities for your spirit guides to lead you forward on a path to a better business. Through the information and exercises in this book, you will be better able to use the energy inherent in your chakras to power your business in a whole new way.

This may require that you crawl as a caterpillar for a time. It will likely mean you will need to spend some time going into a chrysalis of your own making. Ultimately my hope is that, as you read this book, you will consciously change from caterpillar to butterfly and emerge ready to take flight and create the transformation you seek in your business.

ᘓᔖᘗ CHAPTER 1 ᘓᔖᘗ

It's All Energy!

We're all connected. We just don't see it.
There isn't an "out there" and an "in here".
Everything in the Universe is connected.
It is just one energy field.

John Assaraf

Are you open for business? I mean *really* open?

Being "open" for business has a variety of layers. If you're like many business owners, you work hard to do all the things necessary to be open for business but may neglect to pay attention to the energetic interconnection of your actions to your business. On the surface, "open" means you are ready to exchange goods and services with your customers for money. On a deeper level, it means you are open to giving and receiving energetically.

So, let's talk about energy, what it is, and how it affects you. According to quantum physics, everything and everyone in the Universe consists of energy. At the core, we are all made of the same substance. Electricity is energy. The sun is energy. The Internet is energy . . . and you are energy. "Wow!" you say. "She has a lot of energy." Or: "Did you feel the positive energy in that room?"

You exist only as patterns of energy, not as solid matter as you've been led to believe. This means everything in your business is also made of energy – the chair you're sitting in, the computer you work on, the goods and services you sell, the thoughts you think, the feelings you experience, the words you speak, the post you put on Facebook . . . EVERYTHING . . . right down to the last paper clip.

Think back to science class. Remember Einstein's famous equation $E=MC2$? E energy is equal to M mass multiplied by the square of C the speed of light.

To really understand Einstein's equation and how energy and matter are related, we have to dig a little deeper into quantum physics. Research reveals that atoms are actually vortices of energy (not matter at all) that constantly spin and vibrate. Each has its own unique energy branding, just as your business has special branding that lets customers know about your uniqueness. So, neither you nor your physical business exists as matter. You only appear solid because your energy particles vibrate at a slower rate than, for example, radio waves, which vibrate at such a high rate that they can't be seen by the naked eye. Just hook yourself up to an EEG or EKG machine and you will "see" your energy. So, even though you and your business appear as matter, it is all truly invisible energy. And all that other visible matter vibrates at the same speed you do and therefore appears solid to you.

The cool thing about energy is that everyone and everything exchanges energy all the time. Emotions and thoughts vibrate at a higher rate and can't be seen, but you can see the effects of them on yourself and others. In this way, you are sending and receiving emotional and mental energy. There are scientifically calibrated and tested experiments that reveal how energy affects you in real ways. For example, studies show that a negative feeling will cause a muscle to lose 50% of its strength. Furthermore, that same negative feeling can narrow your vision, both your physical eyesight and your mental vision of yourself. In other words, a negative feeling can cause your energy to begin to shut down. Let's demonstrate this to you right now on your own body.

The Muscle Strength Experiment

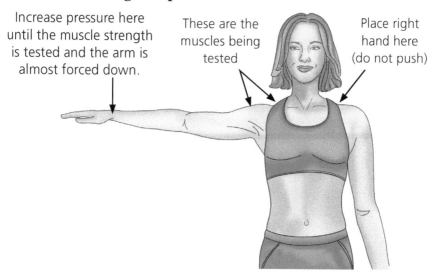

Increase pressure here until the muscle strength is tested and the arm is almost forced down.

These are the muscles being tested

Place right hand here (do not push)

You will need a partner to do this experiment. This exercise may take some practice, so be patient.

1. Let your left arm hang down by your side and raise your right arm until it is shoulder height and the palm of your hand is facing downward toward the floor.

2. Hold a positive thought in your mind.

3. As your partner stands facing you, they rest their right hand on your right shoulder and their open left hand on top of your arm, just above your right wrist.

4. As you hold your positive thought in your mind, your partner exerts moderate, steady pressure downward on your arm while you try to keep your arm at shoulder height.

5. Notice how much force you need to exert to continue to hold your arm up against the pressure your partner is exerting.

6. Drop your arm and take a couple of breaths. Relax.

7. Raise your right arm again until it is shoulder height and the palm of your hand is facing downward toward the floor.

8. This time hold a negative thought in your mind.

9. Repeat steps 3 through 6.

What did you notice? Was it easier for your partner to move your arm while you were thinking the negative thought? Did you notice a difference in how open or shut-down you felt energetically?

Think about this. Have you ever been shut down professionally by someone? What happened to you in that situation? Perhaps they shared some potentially embarrassing information about you, or spoke poorly of you in front of colleagues. You most likely pulled your energy away from that person so you were no longer engaged with them. You might have stopped talking, held your breath momentarily, or even walked away. Physically and mentally you withdrew your energy. Now imagine that you are experiencing this type of constriction continuously while doing your business. Eventually, you will shut down energetically and the energy of your business will be shut down. An example of exactly this kind of energetic shutdown follows.

Rainbow Integrated Healthcare (RIH): A Case Study

Let me introduce you to Megan. She is one of two naturopathic doctors at a small, nonprofit, fast-paced alternative health clinic called Rainbow Integrated Healthcare (RIH). There is an eclectic mix of staff that also includes a psychologist, two massage therapists, two energy healers, an integrative nutrition and lifestyle coach, an acupuncturist, a chiropractor, a marketing developer, and a receptionist/bookkeeper. There is a lot of excitement in the community about the clinic, and patients and donations are flooding in.

In order for RIH to stay competitive in the healthcare marketplace, especially with so many easily accessible traditional healthcare services available to people, three factors are incredibly important – quality compassionate care; customer service; and skilled, knowledgeable, wise healers. In such an eclectic healing environment as RIH, it is imperative that staff be able to engage their own wisdom and creativity so that errors become a learning platform for the improvement of products and services.

Valerie, the other naturopathic doctor (ND), is the founder and CEO of RIH. Unfortunately, she is known to fly off the handle at meetings when "errors" are made, and she regularly knocks down ideas that are not her own. During a staff meeting, Valerie shares that she has received a complaint about the way Megan treated a patient. Without first soliciting Megan's side of the story, she blames Megan and makes insulting remarks about her capabilities.

This leads Megan to withdraw her energy, not only at the staff meeting that day, but also in her daily work from then on. She becomes fearful of incurring Valerie's wrath, as does the rest of the team. The practitioners become mired down in doing things perfectly according to Valerie's standards rather than using their own healing knowledge and wisdom, and this sparks even more complaints from patients.

Valerie continues to act like a tyrant, and the clinic begins to lose its financial base of donors. Cash reserves dwindle. Why? Valerie's excessive anger is causing fear in her staff, and their fear is constricting their energy and shutting them down energetically. In turn, this constricts the overall energetic flow of the organization to such an extent that it eventually starts to shut down both creatively and functionally.

Perhaps you've experienced how a negative thought or event can get lodged in your psyche and affect how you make decisions throughout the day. It can influence how you respond to your customers and employees and what you get done that day.

Let's imagine you're having a particularly bad day. Some of your employees have been cranky. You spilled coffee all over your desk and stained some important papers. Then you find out one of your most loyal customers is going to the competition because they like their service better.

No doubt the loss of a loyal customer will put you into a negative thought spiral that might sound something like this: "Just when I think I'm getting ahead, something bad happens." However, what if this so-called bad thing is just exactly what you need to make the necessary changes to reach the next level in your business? But if you focus on the negative and put that energy into words and actions, you effectively draw negativity to yourself. Energetically, that will bring you more of the same and get in the way of making those important changes for the future of your business.

Certainly you'll need some time to process what has happened. Just don't get stuck there. Approaching the issue with curiosity rather than judgment will help you to reframe the "bad" day as a learning opportunity. Energetically, you open up to learning and creating new ways of doing business and making money. This allows your energy and that of your business to flow instead of shutting down in certain areas or altogether.

The Pendulum Experiment

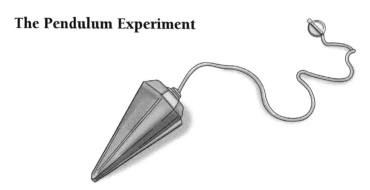

Are you still doubtful that energy operates in this way? Try this pendulum experiment. Pendulums are great for making yes/no decisions and a great way to see energy in action.

1. Take a necklace chain, unhook it, and put a pendant or stone on it so it's attached to just one end. If you have access to a handheld pendulum, that's great too. (These can be purchased at alternative healing stores or Amazon.com.)

2. Clear your mind by focusing on just your breathing for a couple of seconds in order to become relaxed and focused.

3. Hold the end of the necklace/pendulum between your thumb and forefinger with the pendant or stone pointing down.

4. You need to determine the pendulum's energetic signals. Ask a simple yes/no question to which you already know the answer. For example, "Is my name Nanette?"

5. Keep your hand steady, and allow your energy to flow to the pendulum. There's no need for you to move the pendulum; it will move on its own.

6. There are two standard options for a Yes answer from the pendulum – either it will move forward and backward or it will move clockwise. A No answer will be indicated by the pendulum swinging from side to side or counter-clockwise.

7. Practice until you feel confident about the answers. Then you can use it to help you make business decisions.

Pretty awesome, right?

When you start to wrap your mind around the way your energy is connected to everything and everyone, you can begin to understand that whatever energy you put into your business will come back to you.

ᘒᘓᘔᙅ CHAPTER 2 ᘒᘓᘔᙅ

May the Force Be With You

*What lies behind us and what
lies before us are tiny matters
compared to what lies within us.*

Henry S. Haskins

You engage your energy in your business every day as you deal with finances and organizational systems, connect emotionally with customers and business partners, employ your personal power to manifest your goals, communicate your vision and mission to the larger community, and use your gut instincts to make decisions and co-create your business with your Higher Power. These activities require you to apply your energy and are related to the invisible energy centers in your body known as chakras.

Chakras in yoga, certain kinds of meditation, and the Ayurveda tradition are depicted as wheels of energy throughout your body. Indeed, *chakra* is the Sanskrit word for "whee"l or "disk." There are seven main chakras that align with the spine, starting at the base of the spine and ending at the crown of the head. In the chakra system, our invisible energy is called Chi. Chi is your vital life force and is essential for your personal well-being. It is also known as prana, qi and, in the movie *Star Wars*, it is called The Force.

The concept of chakras has been around since at least 500 BC and comes from India. Although the chakra system is an ancient one, modern science is helping us understand how chakras affect us. Studies show that each spinning wheel of energy is associated with a major endocrine gland, which corresponds to large nerve centers in the body. The hormones from these glands regulate our metabolism, growth and development, tissue function, sexual function, reproduction, sleep, and mood (among other things).

Chakra energy expands into your mind, body, and soul and then moves out into the material world. Imbalances in your chakras can turn up in your business in the form of challenges, problems, and obstacles. By evaluating your chakras and the areas of struggle in your business, you can find where you need to balance your chakras to develop new ways of working to create the business you desire.

For example, when you breathe, you take in energy and then expel it. Take a deep breath. Feel your lungs expand as your body receives the oxygen it needs to maintain a healthy system, and then exhale to release carbon dioxide out into the air that is absorbed by plants and trees. With that one act, you are engaged in energy exchange.

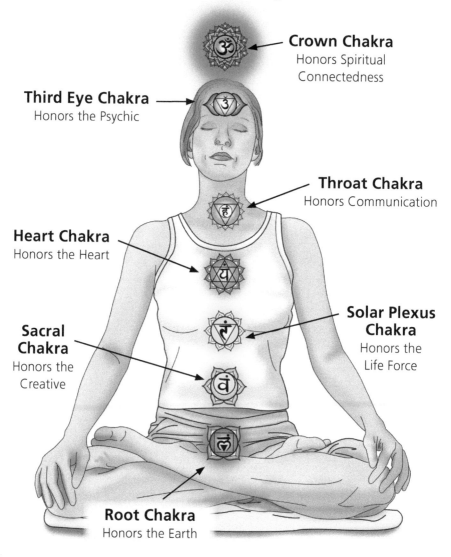

Crown Chakra
Honors Spiritual
Connectedness

Third Eye Chakra
Honors the Psychic

Throat Chakra
Honors Communication

Heart Chakra
Honors the Heart

**Solar Plexus
Chakra**
Honors the
Life Force

**Sacral
Chakra**
Honors the
Creative

Root Chakra
Honors the Earth

Each chakra is associated with a color – red, orange, yellow, green, blue indigo, and violet, forming the colors of the rainbow. Chakra scholar and teacher, Anodea Judith, calls our chakra system the rainbow bridge, which refers to the way the chakras connect throughout the body to make an energetic bridge.

The chakras are where your physical body and consciousness meet. The lower chakras act as conduits to bring earth energy up through your body and connect you with your higher awareness. Your upper chakras bring cosmic consciousness down to help you manifest right actions for the highest good of you, your loved ones, and the world. Ideally, there is consistent energy coursing up and down, and your chakras are clear, balanced, and connected. I call this riding the rainbow, because your energy flows easily and naturally in your body and out into the world in productive ways. However, due to physical, psychological, emotional, social, and spiritual wounding, all of us have imbalances that can show up as disease, crises, and obstacles.

Based on your wounding and other life experiences, your behaviors, thoughts, words, feelings, and desires become your reality without you even being aware of it. Through repetition, your subconscious mind stores these patterns until they become part of your personal programming. Your subconscious mind is the same mind that causes your heart to automatically beat and your lungs to breathe. Habitual responses to experiences determine what your subconscious mind considers true and are the cause of negative behaviors that create imbalances in your chakras.

You subconsciously overcompensate or avoid things to try to balance your energy. If you overcompensate, you create excessive energy in a chakra, and avoidance behaviors lead to deficient energy. In addition, both excessive and deficient energy inhibit the energy flow to your other chakras. By balancing your chakras, you debug your personal programming so that your energy flows out into the world in positive ways. And that is how you help your chakras move towards balance, so your vital life force can freely flow in every aspect of your body, life, and business.

For instance, when you were a child, you may have been scolded when you cried. Over time, this could cause you to constrict the emotional energy in your second chakra (most of your emotional experience is governed by the second chakra), causing a functional deficiency in that chakra to the extent that now you never cry.

On the flip side, perhaps the scolding had the opposite effect on you.

Perhaps it caused you to lose all control and fly into a full-blown temper tantrum. Everyone cleared out of the room when this happened, and even now, you allow your emotions to fly unchecked in the face of everyone. This would be an example of an excessive second chakra that is over-functioning. If the nature of your wounding is particularly harmful, as in the case of abandonment or abuse (physical, psychological, emotional, and/or sexual), this can cause that much more significant constriction or over-expression of your energy.

Similarly, when you eat you bring calories into your body, and they are converted to the energy you need to sustain you physically and mentally. If you routinely don't eat enough, you become underweight, sluggish, tired, and more susceptible to illness. Your body becomes deficient in the energy it needs to stay well. On the flip side, if you routinely overeat, your body will no longer have any place for these excess calories, and you will end up overweight, which may ultimately decrease your physical energy and mobility.

Putting It Into Practice

In the previous story about Rainbow Integrated Healthcare (RIH), the CEO, Valerie, is acting from an excessive second and third chakra. Excessive energy in the form of anger has been stored in Valerie's second chakra. That's because when she was growing up, anger was never allowed to be expressed in her family. To this day, Valerie hasn't learned how to release it in a constructive manner. This dynamic even prevents her from having the space for other, more positive emotions to coexist. So, she lives in a state of perpetual anger that seethes just below the surface. Valerie has so much anger stored that she figuratively boils over, just as a pot that is too full of water literally boils over when it is set on high heat.

The excess energy in Valerie's third chakra (the personal power center) shows up in her desire to control the outcome of all aspects of the clinic. She doesn't share the power, but rather wants to have power over all the others in her organization. Her energy imbalance in this chakra shows up as a business imbalance in the form of limiting her staff's power as they scramble to do her bidding, when their personal power could be better utilized to create and attain goals that support the larger RIH vision and mission.

Chakra Quick Reference Guide

Each chakra has a variety of functions and associations. Some are symbolic; others are physical, mental, emotional, spiritual, and/or energetic. At the beginning of each chapter is a reference guide outlining these correlations. It will help you gain perspective on the different aspects of the chakra and help you balance it.

Below is a Key to the Chakra Quick Reference Guide to help you better understand what the correlations are and how they might be useful to you on your journey.

KEY TO THE CHAKRA QUICK REFERENCE GUIDE

CHAKRA	CORRELATIONS
Sanskrit Name	Sanskrit is an ancient Indic language of India in which the Hindu scriptures and classical Indian epic poems are written and from which many northern Indian languages are derived. Because the chakra energy was most likely first discovered and studied by Indian practitioners of Ayurveda (the traditional Hindu system of medicine), each chakra carries a name in Sanskrit.
Meaning	The translation of the chakra's Sanskrit name, which also indicates its primary function. For example, the first chakra is the Root Chakra, and its primary function is related to being energetically rooted or grounded.
Location	If you draw a vertical line midway through the body, the seven major chakras are located along this midline. Each chakra is associated with a specific location. Other, smaller chakras can be found in the palms of the hands and

	the soles of the feet. One chakra also exists above the crown of the head and one is below the feet – sometimes called the Soul Star Chakra and Earth Star Chakra, respectively. Six of the seven in-body chakras attach at the specific chakra locations along the spine and spiral out in a conical fashion from the front and back of the body. The front side of a chakra spins clockwise and is related to the conscious self and day-to-day reality. The back side of a chakra spins counterclockwise and is associated with the unconscious self and expansive reality, such as past lives and other dimensions. The Crown Chakra only has a backside that spirals upward from the crown of the head and opens up to universal energy and divine consciousness. It also channels Kundalini energy up from the base of the spine through the crown of the head.
In the Body Governs	Each chakra strongly influences the health and wellness of specific body parts, organs, and other physical and emotional systems.
Endocrine Gland	Each chakra is associated with a specific gland, which, in turn, governs various physical, mental, and emotional systems in the body.
Imbalances	When a chakra is out of balance (either carrying too little or too much energy), the imbalance can manifest in a variety of physical, mental, emotional, spiritual, and energetic symptoms.
Energetic Goals	Each chakra is associated with a specific energetic goal. Working towards the goal will help bring greater harmony and success in life, business, relationships, and spiritual connection.

Rights	Humans have innate rights given to them at birth by Spirit. Each chakra is associated with a divine right. Practicing this right using affirmations and actions leads to greater chakra balance.
Color	A color is associated with each chakra. If the chakra is healthy and balanced, it energetically emits a clear, bright color. If it isn't healthy or is imbalanced, its color may appear dim, very light, muddy, or very dark. While they are invisible to most, some people can actually see chakra colors.
Food	The consumption of certain foods will help rebalance and re-energize each chakra.
Element	Each chakra is associated with an element symbolically and energetically. Engaging in the properties of the element physically, mentally, and spiritually will help balance the chakra.
Stones	Certain crystals and stones have been discovered to be useful in rebalancing and reenergizing the chakra energy centers. In addition, they are used to heal issues associated with the chakra.
Animal	Symbolically the chakra animal draws on the larger universal consciousness. Tapping into the animal symbol through meditation, imagining, dreaming, or other creative acts can help balance the chakra.
Archetype	The chakra archetype energetically taps into the greater universal consciousness. Through meditation, imagining, dreaming, or other creative acts, one can mentally embody the archetype and bring it to life energetically to help balance the chakra.

Plant	Whether grown in a garden, at home, or in the office, the visual beauty, pleasant aroma, and energetic quality of the plant associated with the chakra can help balance the chakra physically, mentally, emotionally, and spiritually.
Music	The associated musical note vibrates at the same frequency as the chakra energetically. Listening to music based in that note can help balance and harmonize the chakra.
Essential Oil	Essential oils have chakra healing and balancing properties. Diffusing, inhaling, or applying them topically on the body can help solve physical, mental, emotional, and energetic issues.

Let's take a closer look at each chakra individually and see how they may be directly affecting your life and business.

❧ CHAPTER 3 ☙

First Chakra: Getting Rooted

*"When one has taken root, one
puts out branches."*

Jules Verne

CHAKRA 1 QUICK REFERENCE GUIDE

FIRST CHAKRA	CORRELATIONS
Sanskrit Name	Muladhara
Meaning	Root
Location	Base of the spine
In the Body Governs	Blood, bones, immune system, colon, rectum, legs, feet, large intestine
Endocrine Gland	Adrenals, which regulate metabolism and balance salt, potassium and water in the body; they fuel the immune system, sexual function, and cortisol (stress hormone) production
Imbalances	Obesity, hemorrhoids, constipation, colon cancer, sciatica, eating disorders, knee trouble, bone disorders, frequent illness, frequent fears, excessive worry, inability to focus or be still
Energetic Goals	Safety, security, belonging, health, shelter, work, home, and money
Rights	I have or I need
Color	Bright red
Food	Root vegetables, meat, nuts, and red-colored foods, like apples, pomegranates, and cherries
Element	Earth
Stones	Garnet, ruby, or bloodstone
Animal	Elephant, ox, or bull
Archetype	Gaia, Earth Mother, symbolized by the tree

Plant	Sage
Music	Musical note C and drumming
Essential Oil	Cedar wood, cinnamon, garlic, sandalwood

Deep roots help a tree grow on many levels. They bring water and nutrients from the earth to feed the tree, and they also help the tree withstand wind and weather by keeping it stable. If a tree has a shallow root system, it is less likely to survive. Your first chakra is like the root system of your body, your life, and your business. Indeed, it is called the Root Chakra and is aptly located at the base of the spine.

In your business, think of the first chakra in terms of having a firm foundation. It corresponds to your ability to create a stable, sustainable, and environmentally sound business that is profitable and has good cash flow. You want it to be well organized, with basic structures and systems in place that will support your business now and in the future. The first chakra addresses safety, regulations, policy and procedures, insurance, legal structure, accounting systems, and other basics.

I know! It's not very sexy stuff, and for most of us is definitely not the reason we go into business, but it's very important all the same. In terms of your body, what happens if you have problems with your foundation, for example, your legs? Most likely, you will have difficulty getting your legs under you to stand up and then trouble getting where you want to go even after you've stood up.

Similarly, without your business foundation in place, it will be more of a challenge to get established and then "stand up" and manifest your goals. Many times, you may get all excited about what you are doing and get ahead of yourself before you have the basics in place. Conversely, you may discover that working on establishing a healthy first chakra for your business is more exciting and rewarding than you had anticipated, and that you end up experiencing a newfound confidence and power in yourself and your business. In any case, energetically, when you put a firm foundation under you, it tells the Universe that you are serious and ready to do the hard work necessary to grow a business.

An apple tree can't grow beautiful, leafy branches without roots, and it can't produce big, luscious, juicy fruit before its roots are firmly established. This is true for your business as well, especially when it comes to having and generating enough money to allow your business to establish itself. Having systems in place for accounting and to manage inventory, track client communications, record your time and that of your employees, maintain a client database, evaluate performance, etc., is important. Systems such as these help you build your business foundation.

I correlate this with the first chakra element, earth. Earth energy is very grounded, and roots grow down deep into the ground when the soil is healthy. The earth has four major natural systems – rock, water, air, and life – that are also known as, respectively, the geosphere, hydrosphere, atmosphere, and biosphere. When these systems are in balance, the earth and all its inhabitants thrive. When they are out of balance, the earth gets sick.

Unfortunately, that is where we find ourselves today with all the current concerns we have about planetwide climate change, the extinction of plants and animals, and food shortages. You have only to listen to the news to understand the importance of sinking the metaphorical roots of your business into healthy, well-prepared soil so that they grow deep and provide the stability your business needs to grow and flourish.

Imagine your body as Gaia, the Greek name for the Earth Mother. Your physical body lives on Planet Earth. Earth's gravity keeps you from floating off into space. Central to your well-being is your physical health. In your body, you have systems that include a structure of bones (similar to rock). You also are made of water that you take in through your digestive system, and you breathe air using your respiratory system. You support life – your own and the lives of other small organisms. When your systems are functioning at their best, you feel fabulous. You have energy, you are strong, you are at the top of your game. And like the earth, when your physical systems get out of balance, your health suffers.

Your business is no different. The right systems promote a healthy business. What are the right systems to safeguard the well-being of your business will vary depending on your particular enterprise.

Building on Bedrock

The first natural earth system is rock. Bedrock is the solid, stable rock underlying the looser soil, and it forms the basis for new soil. A tree sends its roots deep into the soil seeking the nutrients it needs to grow strong and lush. Energetically, having the right space and infrastructure creates the bedrock that supports the soil for growing the deep roots needed for your business to be fruitful.

Imagine you plan to plant a small apple orchard. You want to be sure you have the perfect spot for it, with adequate sunlight, rich soil, and easy access. You are going to need the right equipment to take care of the trees, like pruners, ladders, and a means of keeping pests away. All of these things will help form the bedrock of your orchard.

In the business world, bedrock consists of the fundamental systems and principles upon which your business is based. It is the base upon which you build everything else. When you don't put down the bedrock, your business will become anemic and deficient in the energy and nutrients it needs to grow.

Assess the health and balance of the first chakra of your business. Energetically, has your business taken root? Take a look at your workspace, equipment, and infrastructure with fresh eyes. Ask for an objective opinion from a customer or a trusted colleague. Evaluate whether you truly have the bedrock in place to fully support you and your business. Here are some questions to ask and answer.

The space you work in and the infrastructure of your business are the bedrock. What are your needs at this time? It's important to consider the basics, like, price, location, security, physical environment, phones, computers, technology support, transportation needs, furniture, and other equipment. Other first chakra considerations are ambience, amenities, lighting, and storage.

Do you mostly work virtually, or do you require bricks and mortar? Do you and your employees work safely and comfortably? Are the needs of your customers being met? Is your space clean, well organized, and visually pleasing? Are you cramped and in need of more room to grow? Or do you perhaps have too much space? Do you have the equipment you need, too much equipment, or not the right equipment to do the job? Have your needs for space, infrastructure, and equipment changed?

In the Notes section of this chapter, make a list of where you have holes in your bedrock, and prioritize them by order of need. (You will have an opportunity to use this information later in the Taking Action section of this chapter.)

The Grass Is Greener Where You Water

Water is the second natural earth system. Imagine you have now planted that small apple orchard. The trees are young and won't bear fruit this year, but you still need to water them and take care of them. You wouldn't water the soil in your home garden and expect it to somehow get to the orchard. You would need a water source nearby, a means of watering (like a gravity or sprinkling system), and perhaps a vehicle to drive to the orchard and a road for that vehicle to drive on. These are examples of basic organizational systems you would put in place to water your apple trees.

If your space and infrastructure are the bedrock of your business, then organizational systems are akin to watering the topsoil to feed the roots of your business. When water is in short supply, a green, grassy field will quickly turn yellow. In the desert, where there is very little water, life is more difficult to sustain, and there are far fewer plants and animals than in a tropical jungle. Similar to the apple orchard, the field, or the desert, your business has a life of its own, and it will grow more easily with the right organizational systems in place.

Whether you are a solopreneur or have a small business with employees, it is important to have an understanding of how your organization looks. This starts by addressing what kind of business entity will best support you. While this sounds difficult, it really doesn't have to be. The first step is to review the different kinds of business entities: sole proprietor, limited liability company (LLC), cooperative, partnership, S-corporation, corporation, or nonprofit corporation. If this seems daunting, there are free resources you can tap into through the Small Business Administration or SCORE. People there may be able to assist you in making a decision. Having the best business designation helps you determine the best tax structure for your business. It also gives you some protection financially and legally. Equally important, it energetically lets the Universe know you are serious about your business.

Organizational needs also come in the form of regulations, policies, and procedures. Whether they are formally written or not, having some consistent practices when working with employees, customers, and business partners is an excellent idea. Some of these are required by law, as in the posting of labor law posters about OSHA and fair labor laws in the workplace. Others become policies and procedures as you define best practices for your business in your industry.

As you grow, the need for formal written guidelines will most likely grow as well. Ideally, these guidelines are formed in collaboration with the team members using them. Not only will they have the best insights, but they are more likely to incorporate new guidelines if they are involved. At a bare minimum, you need to be clear about your best practices and find a means of communicating them to those who need to know. Perhaps you put them on your website, or, if appropriate, you give them to a customer when you first meet as part of a welcome package.

I find the appropriate communication of guidelines is often an issue for solopreneurs. For example, a massage therapist has a client cancel at the last minute. Does she charge them? Does the client know what the policy is? How has it been communicated? If the massage therapist contracts with a larger organization, a day spa, for example, there would need to be clear, consistent guidelines communicated across the organization as well as to the clients.

If customers know what to expect up front, there is less likelihood of a misunderstanding later. Some of this will be trial and error, as you can't possibly know all the situations that are going to arise in your business, but take some time and consider what kinds of information would be helpful to your customers, employees, and business partners. Most likely, there are already some guidelines out there. There's no need to reinvent the wheel. Google it and adapt what you find to your business.

If your business is a bit larger, you may need an organizational chart and job descriptions to help define roles, establish channels of communication, and clarify lines of authority. Other organizational needs to consider are filing systems (virtual and hard copy), insurance coverage for you, your business, and your space, and a financial system for tracking and reporting cash flow and profits and losses.

Energetically, when you put organizational systems in place, you directly water the business roots you have planted. Without organizational systems, you are expending excess energy. You may become stuck in the same dysfunctional cycles over and over, putting energy in over and over again without any benefit.

With systems in place, you will spend less time repeating information to customers or employees, scrambling to schedule and fill an order, trying to locate that elusive file, worrying about how you are doing financially, wondering if you are getting full tax benefits, etc. When you free up this energy, you will be able to use it elsewhere in your business, perhaps to attract new customers or plant new seeds.

In the Notes section at the end of this chapter, make a list of all the places you can think of where you currently need organizational systems in your business. Prioritize them to be used later during Taking Action to balance the first chakra in your business.

Just Breathe

Air is the third natural system on earth. Water and the particular gases in earth's atmosphere (air) make it possible for life to exist on our planet.

Imagine the apple orchard you planted earlier. Does it have room to expand or are the trees planted too close together? Perhaps, the trees are blowing in the wind unprotected. Do your trees have the ability to breathe?

As a human, you need a steady supply of oxygen to exist. In your business, money is like oxygen. Without it, your business doesn't exist. When you get earnest about money and do the things you need to do to make and spend money successfully, then breathing becomes easier, both figuratively and physically.

When I first started my coaching business, I thought I could put up a website and clients would come. Um, nope! Didn't happen! Prior to that, I had been in management in an established brick-and-mortar healthcare business. Customers came to us. As long as we delivered quality care, we had a steady stream of customers. But the healthcare business is a whole different business model than holistic executive coaching.

I quickly found out I had to get in front of the people who would be potential clients. I had to metaphorically pump oxygen into my business for it to breathe, both in terms of investing my own money and priming the oxygen pump through networking and marketing. Incidentally, I also had to resuscitate it a few times when it was on its death bed.

Statistically, one thing that failing businesses tend to have in common is they don't have the financial resources to allow the business to become sustainable during the first few years. And money falls squarely into the first chakra as an aspect of your survival needs. Even the hippest business in the world is unlikely to be around long without good financial resources.

Your money paradigm is reflected in your root chakra on many energetic levels and therefore also shapes your business. It is directly tied to your feelings about how you think you should make money and your ability to do so. Like air, you can metaphorically breathe in too little or too much money. If you breathe in too little, energetically you will have inadequate money or hold on to money too tightly. Too much may result in excess spending or unwise investments.

Your family history is a good indicator of how money affects your root chakra. While you were growing up, was there a lack of money, overspending, misappropriation, or controlling behaviors by parents or guardians? Or was there plenty of money that was shared freely, invested, saved, and spent wisely? What is your current experience with money? Do you feel capable or inadequate? Do you give up financial power to others or do you take charge? Do you carry a large amount of debt or are you mostly debt-free? Do you feel you never have enough or do you feel you have plenty? What actions do you take when faced with financial challenges? How does this correlate with the financial situation in your business? Do you have breathing room or are you squeezed financially, without the ability to take a deep breath? Look at your profit and loss statement, cash flow, and wages and benefits. Do you feel expansive as you review these indicators of your financial condition, or constricted?

Money Mandala

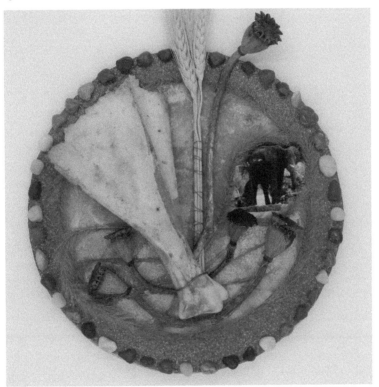

This next exercise will help you discover potential imbalances in your root chakra around money.

Use a template to draw a circle on a blank piece of paper or cardboard. A paper plate, pie tin, or pizza stone will do nicely, depending on how big you want your circle. Cut out the paper circle with scissors or a utility knife if using cardboard. Fill the circle with a red color using a pen, pencil, paint, or marker. This represents your first chakra. Draw, paint, or glue images and symbols within the circle that express how you feel about money.

You may wish to use pictures from magazines or found objects from nature or other sources such as leaves, feathers, seeds, buttons, ribbon, glitter, etc. Use one or more colors. The cardboard works best if you plan on gluing heavier objects on your mandala. Let go of the VOJ (Voice of Judgment) and allow yourself free rein.

This isn't supposed to be a great work of art, just an honest representation of how you feel about money. When you look at your mandala, what do you notice? Does it indicate excessiveness or deficiency regarding money? Or maybe a little of both?

Once you are done, write about your mandala in the Notes section of this chapter. Allow yourself the freedom to write whatever comes to you. Write faster than you can think. Let your hand write the words, instead of your conscious mind. Pay no attention to grammar, punctuation, or spelling, and don't worry about whether it makes sense or not. Continue writing about your mandala until you feel you are done. Then review what you have written.

What insights do you have? How does this relate to the present financial situation in your business? In your life? Does the mandala correlate to any first chakra physical ailments in your body? Keep this information handy for use in the Taking Action section of this chapter.

Energetically, your money attitudes will leak into your business. If you approach your business with a paradigm of lack (i.e., there is not enough to go around), you will have a harder time attracting money into it. If you believe that customers or clients are hard to come by, they will be. If you undervalue your products or services, so will others.

The value of your products or services must start with you. Become aware of your thoughts about how much you feel you can charge for your products or services. Are you undervaluing them? It's possible to overvalue them as well. Be honest. What is a fair value, one that customers will feel great about paying? You may need to do some research in this area about what similar business owners are charging and if customers are buying at that price.

In general, what are your thoughts around money? If you consistently lack prosperous thinking, it's time to do some work around that. When your inner reality becomes more golden, so will your outer reality.

Life on Earth

The fourth earth system is life. Remember earlier in the chapter when you imagined your body as Gaia, Mother Earth? Now, take this analogy and apply it to your business. How well does it support you and other humans that "inhabit" it? Essential to your well-being is caring for your physical self. And essential to the well-being of your business is how well you nurture those involved.

As the leader of your business, you set the example. Your well-being and that of others is directly related to your actions or inactions on your business planet. Look at what you can do that will directly impact the well-being of everyone, starting with your physical body. Basic body needs include healthy food, good sleep, adequate exercise, and safe, comfortable working conditions.

You set the standard for health by making sure you are doing the things that support your body, like not overworking yourself or others, taking stretch and exercise breaks, and giving your employees time to do the same. Eat healthy foods and take a real lunch break – no eating at your desk in front of the computer! There are lots of simple changes similar to these that you can make that will increase physical health. Simple, but not always easy. It starts with the desire to be healthy. Then comes the hard work of developing healthy habits, but the effort is definitely worth it!

Practically speaking, your physical health is primary to the health of your business. Without it, the energy you pour into your business will be sub-optimal. When you feel physically sluggish, your actions will lack enthusiasm and focus. When you are tired, you won't make the best decisions. If you are constantly operating on caffeine, you will approach your business with a false sense of high energy that will collapse over time.

In the body, the first chakra is associated with the adrenal glands, which regulate the production of the fight-or-flight hormones of adrenalin, cortisol, and norepinephrine. Constant stress and fear will throw the adrenal glands into an excessive state, which ultimately depletes them and causes fatigue or illness. That is why using fear to motivate yourself or others will backfire in the long run. Too much stress and/or fear, and you may hit the wall or burn out, either of which will suck the energy right out of your business.

A combination of issues such as not having the proper workspace, poor or no organizational systems, money problems, and constant fear or stress is a sure sign that there is an energetic imbalance in the root chakra. Rainbow Integrated Healthcare (RIH) is showing signs of just such an imbalance which may show up on a day-to-day basis.

Putting It Into Practice

At Rainbow Integrated Healthcare (RIH), team members are complaining that they are seeing fewer clients, and Rita, the bookkeeper, states she hasn't received any donations in weeks. RIH has a lovely, well-equipped space, but the rent is high. Without regular donations, it will be nearly impossible to pay. No one seems to know exactly where RIH stands financially. Valerie, the CEO of RIH, rarely runs the numbers. She believes that profit and loss statements are a distraction from her primary work as a naturopathic doctor. They simply don't interest her. Megan is worried that RIH is failing financially, but without any real evidence, she is apprehensive about approaching Valerie.

As if that isn't enough, several of RIH's practitioners have missed work recently due to an intestinal virus. Client appointments have had to be canceled, and this is further impacting the bottom line. Because the team feels continuous fear in the face of Valerie's wrath, their fight-or-flight response is regularly triggered. The constant stress causes adrenal fatigue and increases the likelihood of illness. This is why team members have fallen ill. It's no surprise that the illness is focused in the first chakra (the large intestine and adrenal glands), since safety and security are first chakra concerns, and all the current problems at RIH are negatively impacting the employees' feelings of safety and security.

The lack of financial monitoring, an increased incidence of practitioner illnesses, and decreased funding all contribute to the money concerns at RIH.

Taking Action

Now it's time for you to take action. Carry out the following activities to help you determine what your next steps need to be in order to become rooted in your own business.

1. Take the Chakra Assessment that follows and record your score. Does it indicate a glaring deficit in this chakra or just some tweaking?

2. Answer the Questions for Further Exploration that follow and write down any insights, new ideas, or awareness you may have.

3. Listen to the Getting Rooted guided journey on the website and journal about your experience: www.nanettegiacoma.com/OpenForBusinessBook.

4. Review the information and insights you have gathered from this chapter about the first chakra.

5. Read Ways to Balance Your First Chakra, which follows, and select which things you want to try or make your own list of ideas.

6. From your list, choose 1-3 things you are going to do.

   a.___ What action steps will you take?

   b.___ Do you need help? What kind of help? From whom?

   c.___ When will you start? What is your goal completion date?

   d.___ How will you know you have reached your goal?

FIRST CHAKRA ASSESSMENT

First Chakra	Yes	No	Somewhat
Do you believe your business has a firm foundation?			
Is your business prosperous, with good cash flow?			
Does your business feel stable (i.e., not undergoing major changes)?			
Do you have good accounting, inventory, customer database, time tracking, and other organizational systems in place?			
Do you have the best legal structure in place (LLC, corporation, non-profit, etc.)?			

Do you have the necessary policies, procedures, and regulations in place?			
Are you adequately and appropriately covered by insurance?			
Are you paying yourself and/or employees well with generous benefits?			
Is your business growing sustainably – financially, humanely, and environmentally?			
Do you have the space, infrastructure, and equipment you need?			
Do employees feel safe at work?			
Do you nurture yourself and others?			
Do you have an organizational chart that shows lines of authority, team relationships, and communication channels?			
Do you have job descriptions that help define roles and responsibilities?			
SCORE			

Give yourself 2 points for every Yes, 1 point for every Somewhat, and 0 points for No.

Scale: 4-12 points: Strong need for first chakra balancing

13-20 points: Some first chakra balancing needed

21-28 points: Congratulations! The first chakra of your business is well-balanced.

Questions for Further Exploration

1. How often do you feel concerned about the very survival of your business?

2. How likely is your business to provide your basic life needs such as food, shelter, and clothing? Why or why not?

3. Do you feel safe at work? Under what circumstance do you have concerns about safety?

4. Did you feel safe as a child? Have you experienced trauma, abandonment, hardship, or physical difficulties?

5. Do you currently have physical problems in your first chakra? What are they? What are you doing about them?

6. How was your right "to have" inhibited in your upbringing? How was your survival provided for when you were a child?

7. Do you feel you are in trouble financially either personally or in your business? Why? What are you doing about it?

8. What recent major changes have you had in your life? In your business?

9. How do you self-nurture? Is your diet nutritious? Do you get enough sleep? Do you exercise on a regular basis?

10. How do you nurture the stakeholders in your business? Do you encourage R & R?

11. How much honor and importance do you give to your physical body?

12. How do you honor and support the physical needs of the stakeholders in your business?

13. How do you interfere with meeting your survival needs personally? In your business?

Ways to Balance Your First Chakra

ᕔ Business

❑ Give your work and/or business some focused attention to determine how to increase its ability to provide you with a solid foundation.

❑ Clean and reorganize your desk, storage, or files.

❑ Redecorate your space so it is pleasing to look at.

- ❑ Rearrange your space so work flows more easily.
- ❑ Fix any broken equipment or buy new.
- ❑ Ask for a raise or give raises.
- ❑ Invest some money.
- ❑ Open a savings account.
- ❑ Balance your checkbook monthly.
- ❑ Track your earnings and spending daily.
- ❑ Make a budget.
- ❑ Apply for a loan or pay back a loan.
- ❑ Consolidate your loans.
- ❑ Put the needed systems in place to run a smooth, effective business. For example, accounting, policies and procedures, computer hardware and/or software, etc.
- ❑ Assess your insurance needs and make appropriate adjustments.
- ❑ Review your business's legal status and make needed changes. For example, corporation, S-corporation, LLC, nonprofit, etc.
- ❑ Review your organizational chart and make needed changes and updates.

❦ Body

- ❑ Tend to any nagging disease or physical discomfort by getting a physical exam, Reiki, acupuncture, craniosacral massage, or other body work.
- ❑ Look at your body in a mirror without judgment and with gratitude. Note all it does for you.
- ❑ Get or give hugs. Pets and people work equally well.
- ❑ Pay attention to your diet and make the changes you know you need to. For example, reduce or eliminate sugar.
- ❑ Experiment with a short fast or a detox diet.
- ❑ Eat first chakra foods – root vegetables, meat, nuts, seeds, and naturally red fruits and vegetables.
- ❑ Keep a food journal and look for patterns in your mood and energy that relate to what you eat.
- ❑ Pamper yourself. Give your body a treat. For example, get extra

sleep, take a sauna, get a massage, take a hot bath with essential oils, go out to dinner, or buy new red clothes.

❑ Get more exercise – run, hike, or lift weights.

❑ Dance to drumming music.

❑ Take a Hatha yoga class.

❑ Diffuse, inhale, or use on your body the following essential oils. For the immune system: protective blend, melaleuca, or frankincense. For bones: wintergreen, white fir, or juniper berry.

✑ Emotions

❑ Get or give hugs. Pets and people work equally well.

❑ Get therapy to work on family patterns.

❑ Journal about how you were provided for as a child and how you feel about the people who were responsible.

❑ Write down some needs/wants that are not being met. Choose two to work on.

❑ List your fears and worries. Create affirmations that assert your safety and well-being.

❑ Find a club, group, or other gatherings of like-minded people where you feel you belong.

❑ Diffuse, inhale, or use on your body the following essential oils. Feeling unsafe: reassuring blend or juniper berry. Feeling you don't belong: cedarwood. For insecurity: myrhh.

✑ Energy

❑ Get crystals or first chakra stones and keep them visible where you work.

❑ Be more earth-friendly by recycling, using LED lighting, replacing power-sucking equipment, composting, or carrying out other environmentally friendly activities.

❑ Backpack or take walks in the woods.

❑ Clean up your outdoor space, rake leaves, and pull weeds.

❑ Make a rock garden at work.

❑ Go barefoot.

❑ Write to your congressman about your environmental concerns.

❑ Do a family history.

❑ Do a ritual for your ancestors.

❑ Get therapy to work on family patterns.

❑ Diffuse, inhale, or use on your body the following essential oils: cedar wood, cinnamon, garlic, sandalwood.

❧ Affirmations for the First Chakra

❑ I am safe.

❑ I am grounded.

❑ I am rooted.

❑ I am financially secure.

❑ I have plenty.

❑ I love my body.

❑ I am healthy.

❑ I have what I need.

❑ I am connected to Mother Earth.

Guided Journey: Getting Rooted

Each chapter will have a written version of an audio guided journey that is available on www.nanettegiacoma.com/OpenForBusinessBook. You may choose to read the journey to yourself silently, read it out loud, have a friend read it to you, or record it in your own voice. It is most effective if you can listen to it rather than read it and then do it.

> Imagine you are standing on a sandy red beach. In front of you, the brilliant blue ocean stretches before you. The warm water laps at your toes. The sun is getting low and appears as an enormous red ball sitting on the horizon. To the left, the red beach blazes in the sun, seemingly going on forever. To the right, is an ancient redwood forest with a sandy path that hugs the shoreline for a time before disappearing into the forest.
>
> There is a legend that deep within this ancient forest is an enormous redwood tree called Deep Root. All who reach this tree have the ability to feel deep within themselves and know true grounding.
>
> Begin walking towards the ancient forest. As you do, a breeze stirs the red sand and it swirls around your feet. Walking along the path, hugging the shore, what do you observe? Are there any

animals? People? Flowers? Inhale deeply. What do you smell? Listen. What sounds do you hear?

It isn't long before the path takes a sharp turn at the edge of a cliff and leads into the shadows of the forest. The redwood trees are huge! Dappled light filters through the trees and their needles litter the forest floor. The air is heavy with the scent. Crane your neck upward and seek the treetops.

You stand there for a time, uncertain of how to find the Deep Root. Then you notice a marker on a nearby redwood. What symbol do you find? Walk over to it. As you do, you see another tree marked with the symbol…and another…and another. You continue following these symbols deeper into the forest, further and further from the path.

As you walk, ponder your current relationship with your first chakra. Are you content with who you are? Do you feel safe? Do you worry a lot? Do you have financial trouble? Are you comfortable in your relationship(s)? How self-nurturing are you? How much honor and importance do you give to your physical body?

Lost in your thoughts, you feel rather than see that you are in the presence of the grandmother of all redwoods. As you focus your eyes, you can hardly believe the enormity of the tree standing before you. The trunk is so big, a hundred people could ring it. The deep reddish-brown trunk is gnarled and appears lashed together with great ropes of bark. It towers into the sky as far as you can see. You feel as small as an ant as you walk up to the tree. Nestled within the folds of the trunk you notice butterflies and other creatures of the forest. A great owl, perched on a branch, startles you with a loud hoot, bringing your attention to a door fitted perfectly into the trunk. What does this door look like?

Behind the door lives your Root Chakra Spirit Guide. The one who knows all about you and where you feel grounded in your body and life…and where you don't. Your guide will help you reach wholeness.

Open the door and enter the heart of the tree. Immediately, you see an ever-burning fire at the center of the space. It is warm and inviting. Take a moment to look around. Sitting near the fire is your guide.

Get closer. What does your guide look like? Allow yourself to observe how you feel now that you are near this being. You are invited to sit close to your guide. Instantly, you feel a great grounding sensation, as if growing roots. Sit with this and feel your rootedness. Feel yourself become part of this magnificent tree.

Your roots thrust deeply within the earth. Your body becomes strong and resilient. Your arms, head, and hair move upward, growing into branches and leaves. You are a tree! You are a tree!

As you embrace your rootedness, check in with your sense of self. Are there any things or people in your business or life that you no longer need? If so, prune them. Are you plentiful? If not, water and fertilize yourself. Are you comfortable in your body? Do you feel safe? If there are places that are scarred and wounded, allow your tree bark to fill and heal them.

Connected to this deeply rooted tree you have the power to make yourself whole. You are connected to your deeper self and the earth. You are safe, you have plenty, you are loved, you belong, you are whole. Dwell on your rootedness. Feel your first chakra at the base of your spine. Imagine it as a clear, bright, ruby-red turning wheel. Feel your strength.

Your Root Chakra Spirit Guide has a gift for you to remind you that you are always rooted when you live from the center of your deeper self. What do you receive? Thank your guide and know that the tree Deep Root always lives within you. Gaze into the center fire.

As you look at the flames, the scene shifts until you find yourself back sitting on the sandy red beach, staring at the huge red ball that is the setting sun. Feel the warmth of the setting red sun at the base of your spine. Sense its energy spinning in your first chakra. When you hear the chimes, you will return to ordinary reality.

∼ Notes ∼

❧ Notes ❧

CHAPTER 4

Second Chakra: Go With the Flow

*Nothing is softer or more flexible
than water, yet nothing
can resist it.*

Lao Tzu

CHAKRA 2 QUICK REFERENCE GUIDE

SECOND CHAKRA	CORRELATIONS
Sanskrit Name	Svadhisthana
Meaning	Sweetness
Location	Sacrum – two inches below the belly button
In the Body Governs	Sacrum, sexual and reproductive organs, bladder, bowel, pancreas, parts of lower intestine, pelvis, hips, knees, and lower back
Endocrine Gland	Reproductive glands: ovaries in women and testes in men
Imbalances	Joint stiffness, lower back pain, sexual addiction, sexual anorexia, isolation, emotional instability, emotional numbness, no enthusiasm, no creativity; living out of your head, never allowing the expression of feelings; may lead to anorexia, bulimia, and depression
Energetic Goals	Fluidity, passion, pleasure, beauty, desire, romance, and connection
Rights	I feel, I sense, I discover
Color	Bright orange
Food	Fruit, especially orange fruit: oranges, peaches, apricots, and cantaloupe
Element	Water
Stones	Coral and carnelian
Animal	Fish or alligator
Archetype	Eros, the Greek god of love and passion

Plant	Jasmine
Music	Musical note D
Essential Oil	Wild orange, jasmine, neroli

Water is the element of the second chakra. It can be soft and soothing like sitting in the warmth of a hot spring, or it can be hard and destructive like a tsunami wave. Water takes on the form of the container it sits in, whether that is a teacup, a stony riverbed, a volcanic crater lake, or the vast ocean floor. Yet, when allowed to flow, water also shapes the landscape. Imagine the dramatic depth of the Grand Canyon, carved over millions of years by the flow of water over rock and soil. When water is blocked, it often becomes stagnant. Visualize a low-lying swamp with brackish water and slimy algae.

When the landscape allows, water naturally goes with the flow. What is the natural flow of your business? Do you go with the flow? And, what does *go with the flow* even mean? Some interpret this as being given permission to be carried along in life or business without responsibility, but I think *go with the flow* means to *allow* flow. When working with your second chakra, ask yourself whether you are flowing or stagnant. In particular, do you allow the flow of emotions, passions, pleasures, desires, and a healthy sexual expression? What about your business? Do you allow the flow of emotions, passions, pleasures, and healthy desires in your business?

Like water, your business can get blocked. When blocks come in the form of relationship issues, it is time to look at the flow (or lack thereof) in your second chakra. Relationships are so incredibly important to your personal success and the success of your business. These may come in the form of customers, business partners, networking relationships, employees, or other stake holders. Most important is your relationship with yourself, because ultimately, all relationships are about you.

Why do I say this? Because I believe we are all put on this planet to learn and grow as souls. Every relationship you have is an opportunity to learn something on your soul path. This is just as true for your business relationships. Sometimes these lessons show up as allies, the perfect partner, an employee, or a customer. Other times, they may show up as a challenger who requires you to dig deep and make the changes needed to get to a whole new level of personal or professional success.

Emotions in Motion

At the core of relationships are human emotions, and emotions are one of the main issues of the second chakra. They can be smooth and serene like a forest pond or crash with anger like a rogue wave. When things go awry in a relationship, it frequently means someone got their feelings stepped on in some way. Humans, by nature, are emotional beings. Some wear their heart on their sleeve, while others are like still waters that run deep. Some are open emotionally around people they know well, and closed around those less familiar.

On a practical level, emotions are some of the most powerful motivators out there. Look at the advertising industry and how it continually uses emotions to influence our buying behaviors. Coca-Cola's current slogan is *Taste the Feeling*, which often includes a picture of a slim, sexy woman in a pleasurable situation drinking a bottle of Coke. The message is, if we just drink Coke, we will have similar pleasurable encounters. Of course, the company doesn't mention that in some of their products there is up to 39 grams of sugar per 12-ounce serving. Nor do they mention the health consequences of that much sugar in the body.

We often make purchases based on how a product or service affects us emotionally. You may be using some of these powerful feelings in your own business to attract customers. Have you considered what feelings you want your customers to tap into when they think of your business? If you are in healthcare, you may want them to feel nurtured. A wealth management company might want customers to feel financially safe. An outdoor adventure company may want to invite feelings of excitement.

The intention for how a customer will feel and how she actually feels when she uses your product or service will help or hinder sales. Give some attention to the feelings you want to elicit when customers use your product or services. Then determine whether this is congruent with your customer's actual experience. You may need to survey a few outspoken people to get the information you need.

The emotional climate *in* your business is also critical to your success. Laughter is contagious, and so are negative attitudes. Think for a moment. What is the prevalent mood in your workplace during the day? Passion and happiness, anger and stress, or perhaps something else entirely? Energetically, emotions are like an invisible superpower. If you arrive at work motivated, happy, and full of passion, that will filter into the energetic field of your business and you will attract the same quality of emotions from team members in your organization. You will be met with the emotional vibrational frequency you transmit.

Positive emotions vibrate at a higher frequency than negative emotions. The vibration you put out into your organization will determine if there is a light or heavy mood. Slower energy vibrates with a heaviness that bogs down constructive flow in your business. Conversely, when you vibrate at a higher frequency, you will attract people and situations that flow with productive energy. Positive emotions create the energetic flow for synchronicity, where the right people, situations, and events just show up.

For example, a few years ago I was looking to connect with more people in the holistic wellness field. I happened to go to a Chamber of Commerce event where a local acupuncturist was being awarded the New Business of the Year Award. I was immediately drawn to her energetically and noted her business name so I could make contact with her at some point. I never had a chance to reach out to her because, less than a week later, she contacted my husband via email at our family business, Long Branch School of Maine. He immediately put her in touch with me, and through her I joined a business networking group that has been the catalyst for me to meet many other holistic wellness practitioners. That is synchronicity at work! In the Notes section of this chapter, write down where you are using your higher vibration to bring synchronicity to yourself and your business.

Of course, everyone has negative emotions and faces adversity. For instance, you may have had an angry, very demanding customer who just couldn't be pleased no matter what you did. At the time, you may have swallowed your anger. If unresolved anger is your norm, you could have set yourself up for an energetic imbalance in your second chakra, namely excessive energy. This imbalance might reveal itself when your anger comes out sideways at employees, your spouse, or your children. Your second chakra could also become deficient in energy so that you end up feeling depressed or lack desire without any obvious reason for feeling this way.

As the leader, your mood influences the entire organization. Energetically, this will show up in the culture of your organization. For example, your unprocessed anger from the demanding customer may draw more and more angry customers into your business. As your anger bleeds into the emotional fields of your employees, the prevalent organizational mood may become dark and chase customers away. Team members may approach each other with angry attitudes, or they may shut down altogether and end up communicating minimally or poorly. You will be left with a business of disconnected individuals instead of a team.

In the Notes section of this chapter, make a list of unresolved negative feelings and the situations and/or people associated with them. These may be from yesterday or from your childhood. Notice if there are any themes, for example, anger, depression, or feelings of inferiority. You will have a chance to work on these in the Taking Action section of this chapter.

Equally as important as to taking care of your own emotional well-being, is how well you emotionally support your employees. Creating an emotionally supportive environment for employees will help you flow to success. Employees bring their feelings to work every day, just like you do. Negative emotions like nervousness, fear, or stress may spark conflict, diminish communication, or hinder performance. On the other hand, positive emotions like excitement and happiness can increase productivity, morale, and team cohesion and decrease counterproductive work behaviors like absenteeism and theft of office supplies.

When an employee is struggling emotionally, it will help shift their attitude if they feel supported in their workplace. This is particularly important if an employee is expected to service customers in a friendly, cheerful way that may be in opposition to their mood. True support can be as simple as listening and empathizing. There may or may not be anything you can do to affect your employee's actual situation. However, you might still be able to help indirect way by offering a paid mental health day, for example.

By promoting a caring, supportive organizational culture, you will contribute to your bottom line in direct and indirect ways. You will enjoy the benefit of a committed, satisfied, involved, and motivated team. The positive energy of your team will flow out to your customers, thereby increasing customer satisfaction and improving your profitability. You will find yourself "riding the rainbow" as you connect the vibrant orange emotional energy of the second chakra to the foundation of the bright-red, financially rooted first chakra.

Have you ever walked into a store where it is obvious none of the employees wants to be there? They lack energy and interest. They rarely interact with customers. And when they do, it is often with a poor attitude or only when absolutely necessary. No one seems to care, and their apathy filters into your energetic field. You are unlikely to make a purchase or come back to shop later.

In contrast, there are shops you enter where you are immediately greeted by cheerful, happy-to-be-there employees. You feel good being there and take your time browsing. Eventually, you may purchase something, even though you didn't walk in with that intention initially. The experience makes you feel good, and more than likely you will return to shop there in the future.

Interesting, pleasurable workplaces where successes are celebrated and mistakes are considered learning opportunities help build energetically positive teams. Connection and pleasure are part of an emotionally supportive culture, and both are important parts of building a strong second chakra in your business.

Making opportunities for employees to connect is a great way to encourage second chakra flow. It can be in big ways like celebrating special events and successes, or it can be in small ways like having healthy snacks available in a communal space that allows employees to take breaks when they feel the need. You might invite team members to a bagel breakfast before work once a month. Your type of business will dictate what kind of connection opportunities you want to offer. Ask your team members what they would enjoy.

What about your business? Do you have a supportive, caring culture that encourages honest expression of feelings and engages employees in interesting and pleasurable work? Do you encourage connections, celebrate successes, and use mistakes to learn? How could your culture be better and improve the second chakra flow of your organization?

Mood Mandala

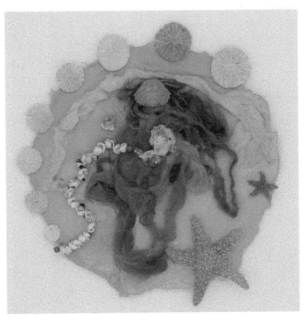

Use a template to draw a circle on a blank piece of paper or cardboard. A paper plate, pie tin, or pizza stone will do nicely, depending on how big you want your circle. Cut out the paper circle with scissors or a utility knife if using cardboard. Fill the circle with an orange color using a pen, pencil, paint, or marker. This represents your second chakra. Draw, paint, or glue images and symbols within the circle that express how you feel about your business.

You may wish to use pictures from magazines or found objects from nature or other sources such as leaves, feathers, seeds, buttons, ribbon, glitter, etc. Use one or more colors. The cardboard works best if you plan on gluing heavier objects on your mandala. Let go of the VOJ (Voice of Judgment) and allow yourself free rein. This is not supposed to be a great work of art, just an honest representation of how you feel about your business at this time.

Once you are done, do some writing about your mandala in the Notes section of this chapter. Allow yourself the freedom to write whatever comes to you. Write faster than you can think. Let your hand write the words, instead of your conscious mind. Pay no attention to grammar, punctuation, or spelling, and don't worry about whether it makes sense or not. Use your imagination. The unconscious mind likes to express itself through the language of symbols and archetypes. Don't edit, don't judge, just write! This is an opportunity for your unconscious mind to tell its story – even if it's, "I don't know what the heck to write." Continue writing about your drawing until you feel you have said what you need to. Then review what you have written. What emotions are most influential? What are the effects of those emotions in your business and your life?

Ride the Wave

Change is like a wave crashing onto the beach. As soon as one wave rolls out, you know another one will come in shortly. At times the ocean is calm and the waves are small and quietly lap at your toes. Other times, the waves are a bit larger, and you may have fun jumping over them. Then there is the thrill of big waves that professional surfers find enthralling. And, unfortunately, there are storms that create waves of destruction and chaos.

Change is inevitable in life and in business. How big are the waves of change in your organization? How well are you riding them? Your ability to make good decisions in your current business climate comes from your ability to ride the waves of change. Consider your business. Do you have the flexibility and creativity to move with the changing landscape? That changing landscape is becoming ever more complex and challenging as the rate of change in the business world increases. It is also exciting and creates oodles of opportunities for the flexible and creative leader. Flexibility and creativity go hand in hand, and both are second chakra matters.

In your body, the second chakra sits two inches below your belly button and is the center of your "gut instincts." Through your second chakra you have the wonderful ability to tie your feelings to your decision-making. This doesn't mean you allow your emotions to run the show. It is about dipping into your center to assess whether a decision "feels" good, bad, right, wrong, or indifferent. As you access your gut instincts, you heighten your awareness of your desires and your senses. This heightened awareness, in turn, leads to creative ways of solving problems and innovative ideas.

The flexibility to allow these new ideas and innovation to flow into your business will facilitate your ability to make the needed changes. Important to this process is having an organizational culture that supports creativity and change. Encouraging your employees to use their mistakes as opportunities to learn rather than occasions for disciplinary action is a great way to stay on top of the wave of change. Creating an open, collaborative, humanistic environment will reduce the fear and safety concerns that keep team members stuck in the first chakra and inhibit the flow of energy into the second chakra.

Remember the children's story of *Stone Soup*? In the beginning, three hungry and destitute travelers came to a village and started a pot of soup with only water and a stone. Initially, the villagers didn't want to help the strangers, but the travelers invited each villager to add a little bit to the pot. Soon they had a delicious, hearty soup that fed the entire village as well as the strangers.

Similarly, you need to encourage team members to feed their passions and add them to your creative business soup. Fostering creativity and personal growth will help your business become more sustainable. It will empower your employees to become the catalysts for change and innovation that will help your business ride the waves of change into the future.

In the Notes section, write about how you approach change in your business. How do you encourage creativity and flexibility in yourself and others?

Passion Plunge

What do you think of when you think of passion? Does it bring up steamy nights of romance and sex? Or maybe it makes you think of creating amazing art, beautiful music, or delectable cuisine. What about your business? Do you have passion for your business? Living and working from your passion, is a second chakra thing. And yes, it includes sex! That same passionate, pleasurable, sensual energy moves out into your life and business as well.

To help with this process, ask yourself the Big Why. Why do you do what you do? Sometimes in the fervor of doing day-to-day business, you can lose track of your why. Your why is the energy directly tied to the passion behind your actions. It is the reason you went into business in the first place. When you are clear about your why, you will be better able to persevere in the face of adversity. You will be more motivated to face challenges head on and come up with solutions to problems. You will also be able to communicate your vision and mission in a strong and inspirational way.

In one or two sentences, quickly write down your Big Why in the Notes section of this chapter. How easy or difficult was it for you to express this? Where do you need to be clearer? What is getting in your way, if anything?

Do you think your Big Why inspires passion in others? How do you convey it to customers, business partners, and employees? Central to this communication is having compelling vision and mission statements. By writing down, focusing in on, and clarifying these statements, you are putting your passion into words that can be shared with the larger organization and community.

Your vision statement not only captures the passion behind your creative idea, but it also requires you to take a leap into the future and define what you want to accomplish. Some vision statements have very specific time frames of five, ten, or more years, while others are more open-ended. For example, Ikea's open-ended vision statement is "To create a better everyday life for the many people."

Your vision statement may be several sentences or barely one. The most important thing is that your statement strongly conveys the passion behind your company's actions, because then that passion will be energetically transmitted out into the Universe. You will be sending an energetic message about your hopes and dreams, to which the Universe will respond. Being crystal clear about your vision will help draw synchronistic events and people to your business.

When your vision is communicated well, it will also inspire other team members. They too will energetically tap into and participate in the larger passion that helps them stay committed to doing the day-to-day work. On a practical level, your vision will drive your goals and the actions needed to reach those goals. It will define what direction you plan to take your business in the future.

Your mission statement tells what your business does, for whom, and how it does it. What is its purpose? This gets to the heart of why someone would buy from you. At this point you are asking customers to quite literally buy into your passion. Indeed, the mission of the organization represents a huge buy-in for all stakeholders. This is where a business has to walk the talk.

For example, Patagonia's mission statement is, "Build the best product, cause no unnecessary harm, use business to inspire, and implement solutions to the environmental crisis." Patagonia is an outdoor clothing company. You might not readily know that from its mission statement. But when you look at how they do business, who they sell to, and why they do it, then the mission statement tells a story of what kind of company they strive to be.

Their business model supports the health of our planet's environment in a multitude of ways. They attract employees and customers who want to make a positive impact on that environment. Ultimately, the positive energy that Patagonia puts into the Universe by virtue of their mission has come back to them in terms of enormous growth in sales.

Do you know your mission? What kind of energy do you want to give and receive? When you reach into your passion center, who do you want to impact? What kind of impact do you want to make? And how do you want to do it?

You may have started with one mission and find you are actually on a different one at this time. You may need to adjust your mission statement, or make one if you don't have one. The creation of your mission statement can be very empowering, not only for yourself, but also for your other stakeholders, because it will help reconnect everyone with what is really central to your business. It helps to maintain an unambiguous energetic path, allowing you and those with whom you work to focus on what's important and let go of what is not.

In the Notes section of this chapter, review your current vision and mission statements and write down some things that need to be revised. If you don't have any statements, write down some preliminary ideas. You may consider including other team members to get some robust input.

Putting It Into Practice

Because of the energetic nature of the chakras, the excessive anger of Valerie, the CEO of Rainbow Integrated Healthcare (RIH), continues to filter into the larger organization, affecting the mood of most team members. They feel increasingly unsettled, and relationships at RIH are strained. Team members are avoiding talking to Valerie and instead are complaining behind her back to Megan. They are angry, and there is an increasing sense of apathy about their work and the organization as a whole. Megan listens patiently but feels she has no real authority to take action.

With negative emotions running high, people are also gossiping in the halls between clients and thereby disrupting the workflow and quality of care. As the organizational mood darkens, the motivation and productivity of team members decline.

RIH started out with strong vision and mission statements developed by Valerie and the twelve members of the Board of Directors. The vision statement reads, "In the next ten years, transform the current disease-center model of healthcare in the tri-county area to a medically integrated, holistic approach that provides optimal health, wellness, and healing." RIH's mission is "To provide measureable optimal health outcomes using an integrative approach that combines the natural wisdom and healing power of the individual and advanced medical technology in a cost-effective way."

These statements were shared with everyone at the RIH grand opening. They were well received and incited community support and excitement throughout the organization. However, both of these heartfelt statements have been all but forgotten. The cohesion and enthusiasm once felt within the organization are rapidly declining.

Up to this point, no one within the organization has been willing to have a frank conversation with Valerie, nor have they alerted the Board of Directors about the situation. Valerie is due to meet with the Board next week, at which time RIH's goals will be reviewed in terms of profitability, regulatory compliance, client outcomes, and client costs. In this meeting, it will become clear how the second chakra energy of each team member has seeped into the greater organizational culture and goals.

In the next chapter, I will talk about how your goals relate to your third chakra and how the rainbow energy of the first two chakras is directly linked to those goals.

Taking Action

Now it's time for you to take action. Carry out the following activities to help you determine what your next steps need to be in order to be able to go with the flow in your business.

1. Take the Chakra Assessment that follows and record your score. Does it indicate a glaring deficit in this chakra or just some tweaking?

2. Answer the Questions for Further Exploration that follow and write down any insights, new ideas, or awareness you may have.

3. Listen to the Sacred Spring guided journey on the website and journal about your experience: www.nanettegiacoma.com/OpenForBusinessBook.

4. Review the information and insights you have gathered from this chapter about the second chakra.

5. Read Ways to Balance Your Second Chakra, which follows, and select which things you want to try or make your own list of ideas.

6. From your list, choose 1-3 things you are going to do.

   a.___ What action steps will you take?

   b.___ Do you need help? What kind of help? From whom?

   c.___ When will you start? What is your goal completion date?

   d.___ How will you know you have reached your goal?

SECOND CHAKRA ASSESSMENT

Second Chakra	Yes	No	Somewhat
Do you feel passion for your business?			
Do your vision and mission statements express your deeper passion, purpose, ethics, and ideals?			

Do you trust your feelings and your "gut instincts" about business decisions, relationships, and needed changes?			
Does your work environment generally have a positive vibe?			
Do you refuse to allow your negative moods or those of others to direct the day's emotional pulse (affect the workflow and attitudes)?			
Are you attracting synchronicity in the form of the best customers, business partners, and employees?			
Do you and others in your organization pursue work that gives pleasure?			
Does the work environment "feel" good? Does it facilitate workflow?			
Are mistakes considered part of the creative learning culture?			
Does your business respond easily to changes and fluctuations during the day and in the larger market?			
Emotionally, are you neither too open nor too closed?			
Do you celebrate and reward yourself and others in your business?			

Do you allow yourself and others in your business to express their authentic feelings?			
Do you mostly approach others from an emotionally balanced place?			
SCORE			

Give yourself 2 points for every Yes, 1 point for every Somewhat, and 0 points for No.

Scale: 4-12 points: Strong need for second chakra balancing
13-20 points: Some second chakra balancing needed
21-28 points: Congratulations! The second chakra of your business is well-balanced.

Questions for Further Exploration

1. What is the fire (passion) in your business belly?

2. In what way do your vision and mission express your deeper passion, purpose, ethics, and ideals? Where do they need to be revised?

3. How and when do you use your gut instinct? Give a few examples.

4. What kind of "vibe" does your business give off? Describe it.

5. Describe your working relationships with others in your business (co-workers, customers, colleagues, other stakeholders). How do you create open and honest working relationships that nurture you and them while honoring the creative talents of all?

6. Describe the kind of business partners and/or employees you are attracting. Are they the best, brightest, and most talented in your field? How do you know?

7. Describe your prevalent mood and the mood of others involved when working in your business.

8. Can team members or business partners rely on each other? Elaborate.

9. Where is the flow in your business working? Where is there no flow?

10. How does your business respond to changes and fluctuations during

the day and in the larger marketplace?

11. Describe any physical issues you have as they relate to issues with joint stiffness, sexual and reproductive organs, bowel, bladder, pancreas, lower intestine, and lower back.

12. Describe any mental/emotional issues you have, for example, anorexia, bulimia, depression, etc.

Ways to Balance Your Second Chakra

◈ Business

- ❑ Write or revise your vision and mission statements.
- ❑ Make your vision and mission statements visible and use them to inspire team members and stakeholders.
- ❑ Have a heart-to-heart with team members and stakeholders about how they feel things are going.
- ❑ Get team members' and stakeholders' honest, anonymous opinions about your organization's culture using Survey Monkey or another survey method.
- ❑ List and prioritize needed changes.
- ❑ Evaluate and improve workflow systems.
- ❑ Give rewards for creative solutions to problems.
- ❑ Give rewards for innovations.
- ❑ Have regular celebrations for business successes.
- ❑ Make your business a learning organization where mistakes are used to create improvements.
- ❑ Create and support a relationship-based organizational culture.
- ❑ Practice relationship-based networking, sales, and marketing.

◈ Body

- ❑ Get a massage or other body work.
- ❑ Get Reiki or other energy healing work done.
- ❑ Take a sensual bath or shower.
- ❑ Swim.
- ❑ Drink lots of water.
- ❑ Eat dark chocolate, at least 80% cacao.
- ❑ Bake and eat bread.

❑ Eat second chakra foods – fruit, especially orange fruit: oranges, peaches, apricots, cantaloupe.

❑ Engage in Tantra Yoga.

❑ Do belly dancing.

❑ Buy and use sex toys.

❑ Diffuse, inhale, or use on your body the following essential oils. For low libido: ylang-ylang or joyful blend. For intestinal support: basil, marjoram, or ginger. For bladder and urinary tract support: sandalwood and thyme.

৵ Emotions

❑ Write about ALL your feelings.

❑ Talk about your feelings with a person with whom you are struggling.

❑ Yell or scream in a secluded place (but not at anyone).

❑ Whack a wall, couch, or floor with a dish towel.

❑ See a counselor or therapist.

❑ Get in touch with your light and dark feelings using a creative process: drawing, painting, writing, music, dancing, etc.

❑ Listen to vibrational music and feel it with your feet, hands, or other body parts.

❑ Create something using a creative, artistic process.

❑ Give voice to your passions through writing or sharing with a friend.

❑ Tell someone you love them.

❑ Play like a child.

❑ Diffuse, inhale, or use on your body the following essential oils. For passion: fennel, jasmine, or inspiring blend. For intimacy: cinnamon or jasmine. For emotional openness: lavender or reassuring blend.

৵ Energy

❑ Wear orange.

❑ Wear or carry coral or carnelian.

❑ Diffuse, inhale, or use on your body the following essential oils: orange, jasmine, or neroli.

- ❏ Do things that give you joy and vitality – eat what you want, get a new haircut, dance, buy new clothes, get intimate, have sex, etc.
- ❏ Bring nature's beauty indoors – plants, table fountain, flowers, etc.
- ❏ Send love notes to people you love.
- ❏ Send appreciation notes to people you appreciate.
- ❏ Completely clean your home and/or business to restore harmony, beauty, and balance.
- ❏ Be a Good Samaritan.
- ❏ Diffuse, inhale, or use on your body the following essential oils: wild orange, jasmine, or neroli.

Affirmations for the Second Chakra

- ❏ I have the right to feel.
- ❏ I fully use all my senses.
- ❏ I embrace new discoveries.
- ❏ I lean into my sensuality and sensitivity to fully celebrate the beauty and harmony in my life and work.
- ❏ I feel great!
- ❏ I discover new ways of being every day.

Guided Journey: Sacred Spring

Imagine yourself in an enormous field of beautiful wild flowers. The flowers stretch out before you on all sides. You stand at the center with the warm sun caressing your skin. You inhale the sweet, heady fragrance and feel happy just to be alive. You glimpse something, sparkling not far in the distance. It dips in and out of view as the flowers sway in the light breeze. Filled with curiosity, you make your way through the field toward it.

As you get closer, you realize it is a tiny stream of crystal clear water. You bend down and drink deeply of the cool liquid. Once you've quenched your thirst, you decide to follow the stream. What do you see as you walk? What sounds do you hear? What do you smell? How do you feel?

You observe that the stream is getting wider. It is now a babbling brook. It sounds joyful, and you feel gratitude walking in its presence. Beneath the crystal water, you see slippery stones and fish darting here and there. Trance-like, you continue walking as the brook continues to widen and deepen. As it does, you delve deeper into yourself and allow your emotions, passions, and desires to bubble to the surface.

After a time, you awaken as if from a dream and notice brilliant orange fire lilies now surround you. You scan the landscape and are startled to find a beautiful sacred spring at your feet, nestled between the flowers. The reflection of the fire lilies dances upon the surface of the water like a thousand fire-breathing dragonflies.

As you stare into the water, you feel pulled to the shimmering depths of the spring. You step into the pool and walk to the center. You walk deeper and deeper and deeper, until you are completely submerged. You aren't bothered by the typical laws of nature and find you can breathe perfectly underwater. The water is comfortable and refreshing. It heightens all your physical sensations and feelings.

Explore this underwater world. What new sensitivities do you feel in your body? What do you see? Hear? Smell? What emotions are immersed in the depths of this sacred spring? Allow yourself to explore your authentic emotions.

You hear faint music vibrating through the water, becoming increasingly louder. It surrounds you like a thousand bubbles, entering your mind, your heart, your every cell until it reaches your soul. Is the tune familiar? It shakes loose all desires, bodily passions, and emotions you may be repressing. What emerges? What have you been denying? What are your prevalent feelings? Are you feeding your passion? What burning desires do you have?

Abruptly the music stops, and in its place Eros (the Greek god of love and passion) appears. What does he look like? Notice his face, hair, and clothes…every detail. He is the keeper of the sacred spring.

All who come to see Him are blessed with inner wisdom, deep love, and the profound ability to see below the surface of their emotions, passions, and desires. Eros invites you to float in the sacred flow of the spring's energy. How does this feel? You experience an intense warm sensation in your abdomen and realize that Eros is filling you with healing energy. What blocks do you release? Where do you sense renewed balance? Where do you receive healing?

You float effortlessly in the healing flow while tiny energy bubbles erupt around you, penetrating every part of your being. In this moment, you fully feel all emotions, all passions, all pleasures, all desires, and the full expression of your creativity and sexuality. A brilliant orange effervescent light encompasses you, igniting the fire in your belly.

At the height of the heat, Eros gently lets go, and you float up, and up, and up...until you softly break the surface of the water. In the next moment, you find that you are lying in the field of fire lilies, which seem even more vibrantly orange than before. In your hand is a gift from Eros. What is it?

You lie still, watching the great orange sun sink below the horizon, leaving a spectacular, fiery sunset that melts into the ocean. Feel the flow of the ocean waves in your second chakra. Deeply experience your emotions, true passions, desires, and the ability to create your own reality. Feel your sacral chakra spinning with bright orange vibrational energy. Be with that fully for a few moments. At the ringing of the chimes, bring your awareness back to ordinary reality.

❧ **Notes** ❧

❦ Notes ❦

◦✄◦ CHAPTER 5 ◦✄◦
Third Chakra: It's Magic

"Unless I have enough personal power to keep commitments in my daily life, I will be unable to wield magical power. To work magic, I need a basic belief in my ability to do things and cause things to happen. That belief is generated and sustained by my daily actions."

Starhawk

CHAKRA 3 QUICK REFERENCE GUIDE

THIRD CHAKRA	CORRELATIONS
Sanskrit Name	Manipura
Meaning	Lustrous gem or lustrous jewel
Location	Solar plexus, between the navel and the base of the sternum
In the Body Governs	Stomach, pancreas, lower intestines, gallbladder, and liver
Endocrine Gland	Pancreas
Imbalances	Digestive problems, ulcers, irritable bowels, excessive weight around middle, addiction, low energy or chronic fatigue, feelings of rage, suppressed anger, a need to be in control or too submissive, co-dependency, workaholism; failure to live up to your true potential/purpose
Energetic Goals	Vitality, strength of will, personal power, sense of purpose, effectiveness; it is your inner adult.
Rights	I act! I choose! I will! I intend!
Color	Bright yellow
Food	Complex carbohydrates – beans, whole grains, and seeds
Element	Fire
Stones	Topaz or amber
Animal	Lion or ram
Archetype	Warrior or magician
Plant	Carnation

Music	Musical note E
Essential Oil	Lemon, lemongrass, peppermint, black pepper

What if you suddenly learned you are a magician instead of an ordinary human being? What if you wielded power beyond your imagination? How would you do things differently?

Magical power is the dynamic energy contained in your third chakra.

The magician is the third chakra archetype and embodies the latent power within you. When you direct the passions and desires of your second chakra into goals and actions, you spark a fire in your third chakra and make magic in your business.

In the 1939 movie *The Wizard of Oz*, the Wizard (aka magician) initially appeared as a big, green, scary head. He used his power to dominate and create fear. Dorothy and her friends were motivated to take dangerous actions in exchange for the things they wanted. But trying to wield power over others is often short-lived, as the Wizard of Oz found out.

The Wizard was ultimately revealed as a fraud. He was just a man standing behind a curtain pretending to be a wizard. He was not using his authentic power. While he did not have the kind of magic Dorothy and her friends had hoped for, the Wizard did have some magic. By helping others to acknowledge the power that lay within themselves, he accessed his true power.

The Wizard gave Scarecrow a diploma, at which point Scarecrow realized he had brains. Lion received a badge of courage and tapped into his inner courage. Tin Man accepted a watch in the shape of a heart, and finally felt his big heart, which had been there all along. Only when the Wizard appeared as his genuine self, was he able to create the magic for others to reach their goals.

Wielding Your Magic

Like the Wizard, you must access your authentic magical powers as a leader. In your business, your true magical powers will shine when you use a combination of your masculine and feminine energies. Masculine and feminine energies correlate with the Taoist concepts of yin and yang. The following is a list of associations of yin and yang.

Yin	Yang
Feminine	Masculine
Contractive	Expansive
Conservative	Demanding
Responsive	Aggressive
Cooperative	Competitive
Intuitive	Rational
Synthesizing	Analytic
Dark	Light
Inward	Outward

In traditional Taoism, yin and yang are considered creative opposites; they are different types of energy. Neither is better or worse; one is not more powerful than the other. Both are important and necessary for balance in our lives, our organizations, and the world at large. As a magician and the leader of your organization, you must discern how and when to use these energies.

Culturally, we have favored masculine energy over feminine. This accounts for the still-prevalent focus on competition over cooperation, knowledge over intuitive wisdom, exploitation of natural resources to secure a bottom line, and so on. Fortunately, there are leaders who are fostering a more balanced approach to power that incorporates both yin and yang energies to support a more sustainable and ethical business model.

As a leader, you wield the ultimate magical power in your organization. Authentic power comes from within you, and formal power from outer sources. You may have formal power in your position as founder, CEO, or president of your company, but effectively using your power to create magic requires you to reach inside your solar plexus and find the right balance of yin and yang.

Yin and yang help you determine the intensity of the power you use. Fire is the element of the third chakra, and like the flame under a cauldron, if it burns to too high, you may burn your magical potion; too low and your potion won't get done at all. Similarly, if you use your power to motivate through fear (high heat), you are likely to get burned. Fear as a motivator can produce results in the short run but rarely produces the best results in the long run.

Fear frequently builds resentment among employees, and ultimately goal attainment suffers as a result. On the flip side, if employees and other stakeholders perceive you as having little personal power (low heat), you will not gain their respect, and it will also negatively impact your ability to reach your goals.

Every situation, person, and transaction requires you to balance your yin and yang power. For example, imagine you have a smart, creative Director of Innovation. You value her immensely, but unfortunately she has an absenteeism problem. No doubt, you wish you had a magic wand, and -poof- she would be at work whenever you needed her. Yet, true magical power doesn't try to control others. It co-creates powerful relationships with others.

In this situation, you will most likely use a combination of your personal and formal power in a balance of yin and yang. Especially if you are angry, you may want to bank your third chakra fire a bit by accessing your yin energy and going inward, using meditation or some other centering technique. This will help you get in touch with your intuitive wisdom about the Director of Innovation and how to approach her collaboratively rather than from a demanding or aggressive place.

Using your yang energy and considering the situation, using rational-analytic data, will strengthen your conversation with her. This may include information about how her absences affect morale in her department and data on how progress on goals is getting derailed.

Because you did the inner yin work, you are able to approach your conversation with the Director of Innovation from a place of curiosity. You ask questions that invite her to share what is going on versus demanding to know why she is absent so much. You find out that her spouse has inoperable stage 4 cancer, and she is trying to hold her career steady and spend precious time with her spouse. With this information, you collaboratively work out a schedule that will benefit both of you.

There are definitely reasons to dip into the masculine energy of yang and make some seemingly aggressive decisions – for instance, if there is an immediate threat to your business or to people in your business. In a situation that requires immediate attention, you may need to make some snap decisions that demand all employees step up and do what you ask.

There may also be times where you have tried to work collaboratively with a person, only to later find they have not held up their end of the bargain. At those times, it may be for the highest good of all to part ways. There might be a mutual agreement to part, they may resign, or you could use your formal power to fire them. Every situation is unique. The point is, you need to determine how to wield your magical power and how to balance the yin and yang within for the best outcome.

Do you feel your genuine personal power? Are you using your power ethically? Is your power balanced, utilizing both yin and yang energies? When your power comes from your solar plexus in a balanced way, you won't need to control others or feel the need to have power over others.

Magic Mandala

Use a template to draw a circle on a blank piece of paper or cardboard. A paper plate, pie tin, or pizza stone will do nicely, depending on how big you want your circle. Cut out the paper circle with scissors or a utility knife if using cardboard. Fill the circle with a yellow color using a pen, pencil, paint, or marker. This represents your third chakra. Think about the percentage of yin versus yang energy you use in your business. Turn your circle into a pie chart that reflects those percentages. For example, you may have a pie chart that reflects 50% yin and 50% yang or 25% yin and 75% yang or 10% yang and 90% yin.

Draw, paint, or glue images and symbols within the circle that express how you use yin power in the yin portion of your chart. You may wish to use pictures from magazines or found objects from nature or other sources such as leaves, feathers, seeds, buttons, ribbon, glitter, etc. Use one or more colors. The cardboard works best if you plan on gluing heavier objects on your mandala. Now do the same for the yang portion of your chart.

Let go of the VOJ (Voice of Judgment) and allow yourself free rein. This is not supposed to be a great work of art, just an honest representation of how you use yin and yang power in your business at this time.

Once you are done, write about your mandala in the Notes section of this chapter. Allow yourself the freedom to write whatever comes to you. Write faster than you can think. Let your hand write the words, instead of your conscious mind. Pay no attention to grammar, punctuation, or spelling, and don't worry about whether it makes sense or not. Continue writing about your drawing until you feel you have said what you need to. Then review what you have written.

How influential are yin and yang power in your business? Do you find you use one more than the other? Why? What are the effects of how you use power in your business? Keep this information handy for use in the Taking Action section of this chapter.

Good Magic

"Are you a good witch or a bad witch?" Glenda the Good Witch, asks Dorothy in *The Wizard of Oz*. While Dorothy claims not to be a witch at all, she certainly has the ability to do good magic. As a business leader, you too have the ability to do good magic in the world. Good magic starts with your core values.

Think about the core of your body, your solar plexus, where your third chakra resides. The benefits of having a strong physical core are back pain prevention, organ protection, good posture, less weight around the middle, injury prevention, and overall muscle stability. You have higher energy and feel more powerful with a strong physical core.

In your business, you also need a strong core in the form of core values. Core values create a powerful, supportive platform for your business. They are the guiding principles for your organization and often drive the operations. Core values are the fundamental beliefs that underpin your organizational identity and help determine if you are on the right path. They help you make the BIG decisions, as well, as steer everyday actions.

Patagonia, the American company that sells sustainable outdoor clothing, is considered a "values-driven" company.[i] Their four core values are:
- Quality (the pursuit of ever greater quality in everything they do)
- Integrity (relationships built on integrity and respect)
- Environmentalism (serve as a catalyst for personal and corporate action)
- Not bound by convention (success and much of the fun lies in developing innovative ways of doing things)

Patagonia embraces its core values by creating a culture that expects employees to produce world-class products. Its leaders nurture their workforce and hire employees who are enthusiastic about innovation, their products, sports, and the environment. They even encourage employees to participate in environmental projects outside of the company. Patagonia is taking the high road. Its core values are the catalyst for its greater goals and actions.

Like the Yellow Brick Road, your core values provide a step-by-step guide on the high road to the Emerald City, a place of prosperity, community, and cooperation. When you take the path for the highest good of all, you will find the deeper resources to overcome obstacles and make mindful decisions that will benefit your business, your employees, your stakeholders, and the greater world.

Your core values will also help you find like-minded souls to walk with you. Dorothy's fellow travelers were the Tin Man, Lion, and Scarecrow. How about you? What kind of people do you want to accompany you on your business journey? Do you have core values that attract these people? Do you help them attain their goals while walking towards your business goals? How do your hiring practices reflect this?

What core values currently drive you personally? Are they the same or different from the core values that drive your business? Do you invite others in your organization to participate in the core values? Finally, how are you walking your Yellow Brick Road to the Emerald City?

In the Notes section of this chapter, review your core values statement and write down anything that needs revision. If you don't have any written core values, write down some preliminary ideas. You may consider including other stakeholders in this exercise and listen to what values are important them.

The Magic of Goals

Dorothy, using the magical power of the ruby slippers, finally reaches her goal (home). Her plan often didn't work out the way she thought it would, and she had to make difficult decisions along the Yellow Brick Road, but most importantly she kept walking toward her goal, while keeping her core values intact in the face of challenges.

When you connect your goals with your core values, you wear your own pair of ruby slippers. The ruby slippers represent how you walk the talk (take action) on your core values (your Yellow Brick Road). Dorothy was very clear about her goal of getting home, and she persevered in the face of great obstacles.

Dorothy's perseverance is related to the inherent rights correlated with the third chakra: I act! I choose! I will! I intend! As your magical powerhouse, your third chakra helps you stay the path to reach your goals. It gives you the strength to get up, again and again, when the flying monkeys come for you. It helps you choose wisely when you feel imprisoned in a situation. It helps you take action in the face of adversity and uncertainty. Ultimately, your third chakra helps you take your vision, mission, and core values and move them into actionable steps toward your goals.

Your first magical step along your Yellow Brick Road is to make some goals. SMART goals are a great way to get focused and track your progress. SMART is an acronym that stands for **S**pecific, **M**easurable, **A**ttainable, **R**elevant, and **T**ime bound. Unless, you have these elements in your goals, it will be difficult to determine who is involved, what needs to be done, what action steps to take, and when you will get there. Also, remember that your goals should embody your vision, mission, and core values. Below are examples of SMART goals for Rainbow Integrated Healthcare.

RIH Short-Term Goals
- Goal 1 – Financial
  RIH will increase after-tax profits by 10 percent by the end of the current fiscal year.

- Goal 2 – Marketing and Sales
  Launch holistic women's health services by the end of the current fiscal year.
- Goal 3 – Human Resources
  Increase continuing education for all staff to twenty-four hours per person by the end of the current fiscal year.
- Goal 4 – Operations
  By the end of the current fiscal year, increase billable hours by 5 percent while improving medical outcomes by 10 percent.
- Goal 5 – Community
  Host a community luncheon two times annually by the end of the current fiscal year.

Goals that are irrelevant or feel unattainable will result in poor goal attainment. On the flip side, you don't want goals that are too easy. They need to be difficult enough that you and your employees feel challenged. Additionally, when employees feel that goals are meaningful and within their control, they usually are more motivated to reach the goals. Giving routine feedback on progress also leads to higher goal attainment.

In the Notes section of this chapter, review your current goals in terms of how SMART they are. Adjust your goals where needed. If you don't have goals, write down some current objectives that you will turn into SMART goals. Consider including other team members in the process of setting long-term and short-term goals for your organization. You will end up with a strong set of meaningful goals that team members will feel more motivated to attain.

Flying Monkeys

Once you have your SMART goals, you are ready to take action steps on your Yellow Brick Road to reach the Emerald City and ultimately your goals. Unfortunately, the road to success is not always easy. Like the flying monkeys that descended upon Dorothy and her friends, temporarily interrupting their progress, obstacles may descend upon you and interfere with your goal attainment.

They may take the form of external issues, like rival goals, organizational weaknesses, competition, economic climate, or a myriad of other concerns. Commonly, there are deeply personal obstacles that need to be overcome as well. This may be at the individual level or organizational level.

For instance, you may have a general lack of confidence that leaves you immobile when faced with external obstacles. Perhaps there is an organization-wide fear of change that leaves everyone paralyzed, unable to take the steps needed to reach the goals. In these instances, you and/or your organization may be acting out of a deficient third chakra. Your power center doesn't have the fire to see you through the obstacles.

On the flip side, there may be an excessive third chakra. One individual may consume the organizational fire by wielding their power in ways that leave team members disempowered and unmotivated. In other instances, there may be negative interdepartmental politics that lead to power struggles, which will ultimately derail goal attainment.

So, what do you do when the flying monkeys come? The first step is to name the flying monkeys. In other words, identify your obstacles.

The following is a technique developed by the CEO of Body Mind Health, Alison van Zandbergen, and her associate Ann Washburn.

Overcoming Obstacles Exercise

1. In the Notes section of this chapter, draw a stick figure on the far left of the page. To the right of it draw five vertical lines. To the far right of the lines, draw a star.

2. The stick figure is you or your business. The vertical lines are your obstacles. The star is your goal.

3. Write your name or the name of your business under your stick figure.

4. Write down your SMART goal that you are working on under your star.

5. Below your drawing, write down each obstacle – a, b, c, d, e.

6. An example of business obstacles might be:
   a. There are too many competing agendas and too much office politics.
   b. People are mired in how things have been done in the past.

7. An example of a more personal obstacles might be:
   a. I lack self-confidence to reach my business goal.
   b. I don't feel I have the authority to make needed changes to reach my business goal.

8. For each obstacle, write down what you need to do to overcome your obstacle. For example, for the obstacle in 6.b above (People are mired down in how things have been done in the past), you might write down the following:

   a. Set up a program that rewards team members for creating new solutions to old problems.

   b. Recognize and reward individuals and teams for reaching benchmarks toward the goal.

9. Each action can be transferred to the Tracking Form, which can be downloaded at www.nanettegiacoma.com/OpenForBusinessBook.

This exercise is a great way to get your right and left brain working together to overcome your obstacles. The results can then be incorporated into action steps that will help you reach your goal.

Putting It Into Practice

It is time for Rainbow Integrated Health's quarterly board meeting. Susan, the chair of the Board of Directors, has been hearing some grumblings in the community about RIH, which leads her to invite the entire RIH team to the meeting. Susan is a retired hospital administrator, with over 30 years of experience in healthcare.

Other board members include a doctor, an RN, a CPA, a lawyer, a grants writer, and a marketing and sales manager. Other interested community members on the board are a mother, a father, two senior citizens, and a college student. With the twelve members of the board and the twelve members of RIH, there are twenty-four people at the meeting.

On the agenda are the following: financial report, client outcomes, customer satisfaction, regulatory compliance, and goals. Susan gets right down to business, asking for the financial report. Howard, the CPA and the board treasurer, shares the profit and loss statement, which shows a sharp decline in profits over last month, mostly due to a decrease in billable client hours. The balance sheet shows that cash reserves are declining as well.

Fatimah, RN, and José, MD, are the volunteer quality assurance specialists for RIH. They monitor client outcomes and regulatory compliance issues. José reports that regulatory compliance is fantastic, as are client outcomes, which have improved by 5% since RIH started. Despite this assessment, Devon, the volunteer board marketing and sales manager, reports that customer satisfaction has declined over the last month by 25% according to online surveys sent out after every client wellness session.

Susan then checks in with Valerie, ND and CEO of RIH, on the progress toward the remaining goals. Valerie reports that there is a community luncheon scheduled for the third Friday of next month. While there is still some preparation to be done, she knows they will be ready.

Valerie admits to having difficulty hiring a holistic women's healthcare professional. She has interviewed a few nurse practitioners, who are also midwives, but doesn't like any of them. There is still nine months before the end of the fiscal year, so Valerie states she isn't worried.

While glowering at the other team members, Valerie then relays that no one has come to any of the Lunch and Learn continuing education opportunities that Valerie herself is teaching. So there has been no progress on the 24 hours of continuing education for team members for the year.

Susan and the other board members are concerned about the current financial, customer satisfaction, and education trends at RIH. Susan asks for comments and suggestions from the twelve RIH team members. She is met with fidgeting, downcast eyes, and silence from most.

Megan, the other naturopathic doctor, clears her throat and tentatively shares her observations about the reasons for the poor performance on these goals. In her opinion, there is growing discontent among the team members at RIH, resulting in a lack of motivation and participation in reaching the goals. She continues that, for her part, she doesn't feel like she has the authority to make the best wellness decisions that will ultimately support RIH's goals. All eyes turn to Valerie, whose face has turned bright red. She looks like she is about to fly into a fit of rage, a reaction well known to the other RIH team members.

At RIH, the collective third chakra power of the team has been repressed in fear of Valerie's frequent rages. While the entire team deeply feels the vision, mission, core values, and goals are meaningful, they don't feel they have the control to take action on the goals in ways that are authentic and personally empowering. This has negatively impacted the team's motivation, has impeded their professional abilities, and has created distractions from the goals, all of which has resulted in overall poor goal performance at RIH for the first quarter.

Taking Action

Now it's time for you to take action. Carry out the following activities to help you determine what your next steps need to be in order for you to be able to appropriately harness and exercise the third chakra power of your business.

1. Take the Chakra Assessment that follows and record your score. Does it indicate a glaring deficit in this chakra or just some tweaking?

2. Answer the Questions for Further Exploration that follows and write down any insights, new ideas, or awareness you may have.

3. Listen to the Power of the Lioness guided journey on the website and journal about your experience: www.nanettegiacoma.com/OpenForBusinessBook.

4. Review the information and insights you have gathered from this chapter about the third chakra.

5. Read Ways to Balance Your third chakra, which follows and select which things you want to try or make your own list of ideas.

6. From your list, choose 1-3 things you are going to do.

    e.___ What action steps will you take?

    f.___ Do you need help? What kind of help? From whom?

    g.___ When will you start? What is your goal completion date?

    h.___ How will you know you have reached your goal?

THIRD CHAKRA ASSESSMENT

Third Chakra	Yes	No	Somewhat
Do you feel powerful?			
Is your inner Magician-in-Chief balanced in yin and yang energy?			
Do you share power in your business with other stakeholders?			
Do you have a clear idea about what your business is and what it isn't?			
Do you have written core values that drive the actions of your business?			
Can you say no to things that aren't in alignment with your business path?			
Do you have SMART goals to which you are committed?			
Do you achieve most of your goals?			
Are you mostly satisfied with your business decisions and those of other team members?			
Do you routinely encourage team members to implement their ideas and innovations?			
Are you respected by team members, business partners, and other stakeholders?			

Do team members, customers, and business partners have a positive view of the leadership in your business?			
Are the expectations for hours worked per week for yourself and others reasonable and sustainable?			
Do you encourage periods of fun and relaxation for yourself and other team members?			
SCORE			

Give yourself 2 points for every Yes, 1 point for every Somewhat, and 0 points for No.

Scale: 4-12 points: Strong need for third chakra balancing
13-20 points: Some third chakra balancing needed
21-28 points: Congratulations! The third chakra of
your business is well-balanced.

Questions for Further Exploration

1. What constitutes power to you?
2. How do you know when you have it?
3. How do you know when someone else has it?
4. When do you feel most powerful? Least?
5. Who in your business (past or present) is powerful in a way you respect? How?
6. How powerful do you feel in your business? At home? Among friends and family?
7. How do you allow others to feel powerful in your business?
8. When and how are you a workaholic or an overachiever?
9. Do you encourage workaholic behavior in your organization? Why or why not?
10. Can you say no easily? If not, why?

11. What are you really committed to in your business right now? What are your goals?

12. Are you easily pulled off course or blocked from your goals? What are the detours, the blocks?

13. Describe any physical issues you may have related to your stomach, pancreas, lower intestines, gallbladder, or liver. For example, digestive problems, ulcers, irritable bowels, excessive weight around middle, addiction, low energy, or chronic fatigue.

14. Describe any mental or emotional issues, for example, feelings of rage, suppressed anger, a need to be in control or too submissive, co-dependency, workaholism, or feelings of failure about living up to your true potential or purpose.

Ways to Balance Your Third Chakra

ᕑ Business

❑ Write or update your core values.

❑ Share your core values with all stakeholders.

❑ Create or update your goals.

❑ Get stakeholders' involvement in creating goals.

❑ Put in a suggestion box and take action on quality suggestions.

❑ Reward the actions of employees that help reach goals.

❑ Encourage work breaks that are fun and relaxing.

❑ Create a culture that prizes a balance of work and personal life.

❑ Create a culture that invites solving problems without management's permission.

ᕑ Body

❑ Do breathing exercises.

❑ Kundalini yoga.

❑ Dance and shake your hips and torso.

❑ Twist your torso, alternating left and right.

❑ Work on strengthening your core.

❑ Do stomach crunches.

❑ Do plank exercises.

❑ Spend 10-20 minutes in the sun daily.

- ❑ Do a 30-day cleansing diet.
- ❑ Eat third chakra foods – complex carbohydrates like beans, whole grains, and seeds.
- ❑ Diffuse or wear the following essential oils. For digestion: peppermint, ginger, digestive blend, or lemon..

❧ Emotions

- ❑ Cross your arms in front of your stomach when interacting with others' negativity.
- ❑ Write down your fears about anger, power, people, or situations in your life.
- ❑ Express your anger – whack a wall with a dishtowel, punch a pillow until you are exhausted, scream to express your anger while alone.
- ❑ Write about any co-dependent behaviors.
- ❑ For feelings of powerlessness diffuse or wear the following essential oils -- clove, ginger, arborvitae, or jasmine.
- ❑ Commit to a mindfulness meditation practice.
- ❑ Write down where you want to create more choice and power in your life.
- ❑ Diffuse or wear the following essential oils. For anger: cardamom, thyme, calming blend. For being overly controlling: cinnamon, wintergreen, sandalwood. For empowerment: arborvitae, ginger, clove.

❧ Energy

- ❑ Wear yellow clothing.
- ❑ Carry/wear amber or topaz.
- ❑ Write down your life mission and goals.
- ❑ Imagine yourself as a lion.
- ❑ Dress up as someone you admire or as a hidden part of yourself.
- ❑ Practice saying no to those you usually say yes to.
- ❑ Mentally and energetically cut the cords with a person who you feel has power over you.
- ❑ Diffuse or wear the following essential oils: lemon, lemongrass, peppermint.

✎ Affirmations for the Third Chakra

- ❑ I have the power to make the best decisions for my life.
- ❑ I am the authority in my life.
- ❑ I do what it takes to succeed.
- ❑ I control my destiny.
- ❑ I take the action needed to reach my goals.
- ❑ I manifest my best business.
- ❑ I embody confidence and balance.
- ❑ I use my power for good.
- ❑ I am free of the need to be in control of everyone and everything in my life.

Guided Journey: Power of the Lioness

I once had a dream about a lioness leaping out of a cave with an indigo door, to land in front of me, and I knew it was an intuitive message for me to fully embody my own power, and to pay attention to how I work with others. The lion is the animal archetype of the third chakra.

In Tarot, the *Strength* card is frequently represented by a woman with a lion. It is all about drawing on your inner strength and power. In ancient Egypt, Sekhmet was a lion-headed goddess who was known as the goddess of fire, war, dance, love, and healing. In Hinduism, the goddess Durga rides a lion as a symbol of her mastery over power, will, and determination.

Symbolically, the lioness is about wisdom, power, courage, conviction, justice, leadership, protection, and love. She is the perfect symbol to help you let go of your lower self and embrace your inner power and authority, while, at the same time seeking to tame the beast within.

> *Imagine you are in the African savanna, standing beneath the umbrella of a large acacia tree. You rest against its small, dark trunk, which supports an amazing number of sparse branches topped by a full head of small green leaves. It is early afternoon, and it is beginning to feel hot. It feels good to rest in the dappled shade.*
>
> *Scan the landscape and notice the tall, yellow grass that stretches out in all directions. Above stretches an expanse of pale blue sky. Dotting the vastness are more acacia trees, small shrubs, and an occasional termite mound. The hot air shimmers so that*

the landscape looks a bit blurred and surreal. Sometimes you think you see a lizard or small snake, but in the next moment, it is gone. You hear the songs of birds and the chatter of monkeys, but they too remain hidden from view.

Reluctantly you set out to find water, as the day will only get hotter and you feel a bit thirsty. As you walk, you can't shake the feeling that you are being watched. Every so often you pause, turn, and look around, but you see nothing. Again, you pause. Then, from the grass emerges the biggest lioness you can imagine. Her yellow body blends with the colors of the savanna grass. Her amber eyes seem to look through you. She purrs loudly and seems very pleased with herself.

It's hard to tell how long you stare at each other, but finally the lioness speaks. "Jambo! Or hello, as you say. My name is Zalika, I am Queen of the Savanna, and I am here to help you. Within you, lies the heart of a lion, but your outer power shows but a flicker of it. You need to allow your third chakra to fully flame in order to own your inner lion. Follow me and I will show you how. By exploring the wild terrain of the savanna, you will find your true power."

You begin your trek, walking unhurriedly beside Zalika. You walk, and walk some more, until you hear a cacophony of monkeys. The lioness saunters directly into a troop of monkeys down on the ground, searching for roots to eat. For a moment, you observe their behavior and interactions. Then the leader comes and greets you. "Jambo! I am Rashidi, and I am here to help you get out of your monkey mind and instead connect to the power of your solar plexus."

With that, he asks you to sit. He holds your head between his tiny paws, and he presses his fuzzy forehead against yours. Instantly you feel thousands of small prickles in your brain. Your brain begins to calm. It releases any restless thoughts. You are fully focused in the present moment when Rashidi pulls away. You are thunderstruck by a rush of energy flowing into your solar plexus. Rashidi looks you in the eye and laughs a deep belly laugh, then scampers away.

Zalika nudges you to standing, and you take up your trek again across the savanna. The lioness purrs as she paces alongside you. It is hot, and you feel thirsty. As if reading your mind, Zalika says, "There is a watering hole just up ahead." As you approach, you see a huge elephant with tough grey skin and enormous tusks.

The elephant approaches and says, "Jambo! I am Ananda, and I will usher you into the power of emotional observation. Come ride on my back. Emotions can carry you to liberty or restriction. To be truly powerful, become a neutral observer of your emotions." Her hypnotic voice puts you into a trance, and you barely register it when she dives below the surface of the water.

Below the water, your emotions drift apart from you and float beside you. Observe them and notice what they are. What do you need to learn from these emotions at this time?

Ananda speaks. "Observing your emotions helps you stay in your power. Take time to allow and observe and become informed by your intense feelings." With that, she surfaces and breaks the trance. She sprays a trunkful of water over both of you. It feels like pure joy!

You slide from Ananda's back. You thank her.

Then you and Zalika continue your journey across the savanna. Before too long, you feel the earth trembling beneath your feet. Something very heavy is running rapidly towards you. You see dust rising above the tall grass. Then you catch a glimpse of an imposing rhinoceros coming at you at full speed. At the sight of its mighty, armored body and impressive horns, a bolt of power surges up through you from the earth. The closer the rhino gets, the steadier your resolve to stand your ground.

A sense of physical strength permeates you to the core. The rhino runs right up to you and stops, snorting and breathing heavily in your face. There you stand, nose-to-nose with the rhino. Even though you know it makes no sense, you feel willing and capable of butting heads with this tank of an animal. He smiles and says, "Jambo! Virang, at your service. Way to embrace your rhino power! True physical power is about maintaining a strong, healthy body, staying grounded, and embodying inner strength." Then with a smile still on his face, Virang turns and trots off into the savanna.

Zalika turns in the opposite direction and quietly saunters through the tall grass toward the setting sun. You run to catch up. You walk for some time, pondering the different lessons of power. Long shadows are beginning to creep across the savanna, and it is slowly getting dark. You are feeling very tired. The only sound is the soft padding of Zalika's paws on the ground. The Lioness directs you to rest under an acacia tree. Soon you are asleep.

You dream that you are standing, watching a pride of lions. As you gaze around you, you see the silhouette of a large lioness walking towards you. It is Zalika, and she appears even more stately and powerful. She comes up to you and breathes on you with her hot, sweet breath. It permeates every cell in your being to your core.

Great heat rises through you and a yellow flame of power ignites in your solar plexus. Feel the energy move through you, connecting your power with your purpose, your goals, and the will to act for the highest good of all. Feel your perfect inner strength and power. Feel at one with the balance of power surging from your solar plexus.

You feel the power in your mind, body, and soul. You notice the shadow of a lioness reflected in the moonlight. It mirrors all your actions. With sudden realization, you see you have become a huge, beautiful, yellow lioness with all the wisdom, courage, balance, authority, and love that comes with true power.

In a few moments, I will ring the chimes, and you will come back to ordinary reality. You will awaken feeling wise, powerful, courageous, filled with conviction, protection, and love. You will be in complete balance. You will have integrated your inner lioness into your life.

∼ Notes ∼

⚬ Notes ⚬

CHAPTER 6

Fourth Chakra: At the Heart of the Matter

Your heart knows the way. Run in that direction.
Starhawk

A grateful heart is a magnet for miracles.
Starhawk

If your goals aren't synced with the substance of your heart, then achieving them won't matter much.
Danielle LaPorte

CHAKRA 4 QUICK REFERENCE GUIDE

FOURTH CHAKRA	CORRELATIONS
Sanskrit Name	Anahata
Meaning	Sound that is made without any two things striking. Also, unhurt, unstuck, fresh, and clean.
Location	Center of the chest
In the Body Governs	Heart, upper chest, upper back, circulation, lungs, breasts, and arteries
Endocrine Gland	Thymus
Imbalances	Heart problems, lung disease/cancer, tuberculosis, arrhythmias, hypertension, asthma and other breathing disorders; poor circulation, breast cancer, collapsed chest, shallow breathing; melancholy, codependency, constant caretaking, or clingy behavior; being too open or too sensitive; living at the whim of others' moods and emotions; low self-esteem; running away from intimacy or pushing people away; paranoia and an inclination toward secrecy and betrayal
Energetic Goals	Balanced in relationships. Self-love. Compassion for self and others. Self-acceptance
Rights	I give, I care, I love
Color	Green, which is the predominant color on earth
Food	Green vegetables like spinach, artichokes, asparagus, broccoli, celery,

	cucumbers, all edible green leaves, and seaweed. Also, green fruit like limes, honeydew melons, kiwi fruit, green grapes, green apples, etc.
Element	Air
Stones	Green jade, rose quartz, or emerald
Animal	Antelope, dove
Archetype	Aphrodite, Christ, and Quan Yin
Plant	Rose, foxglove, or lily
Music	Musical note F
Essential Oil	Rose, geranium, ylang ylang, grounding blend

An open heart means being open to giving and receiving, compassion, gratitude, forgiveness, and love. Ummm – bring love into the workplace? That's just weird! Isn't it? While the heart chakra definitely corresponds to romantic love, I'm referring to the love of all humankind, your larger community, your love of the planet, universal love, and, of course, self-love. It is essential to your well-being and that of your business.

Through your heart chakra, you learn how to be in harmony with others, balance your life and business, and attain a more global perspective. You improve your performance and that of your business as you increase your energetic heart connection with yourself, others, and the greater Universe.

While you might have been taught to put others before yourself, truly you must first have compassion, understanding, and acceptance of yourself before you can share your love with the world. Love begins with you. Ultimately, all relationships are about your relationship with yourself. Others on your life path help you to learn what you need to become whole. Until you come to accept and love yourself unconditionally, you will be acting out of a wounded place in the heart of your small-self.

A good place to start is by acknowledging the parts of yourself that you reject – parts you may hide, even from yourself. Everyone has inborn heart wisdom that is a part of your soul print. Within your heart and soul lie your innate gifts. Throughout life, parents, teachers, friends, employers, society, and others help you define who you are. They give you advice and reflect back to you their expectations and perceptions of reality. As well intentioned as they are, many of them don't know themselves, let alone who you are.

Starting from a very young age, you are led to walk a path other than your own – one that is not based on the wisdom of your own heart. To this day, you may still bury parts of yourself that feel unsafe to express. Layers and layers of social, familial, ancestral, and historical messaging can cause you to hide your soul self.

For instance, as a child you might have squashed your strong opinions for fear of punishment, abandonment, or ridicule. Or you may have been a budding entrepreneur in a family of engineers, where your special talents and perspective were not valued. Additionally, childhood trauma in the form of psychological, emotional, and physical wounding may further cause you to submerge your soul self, until you hardly remember who you are. When you start identifying the hidden parts of yourself, you will begin reclaiming your soul self – your inner wise woman.

In the Notes section that follows, list aspects of yourself that you believe are unacceptable. Perhaps there are things you wish you could change or you have been told by others you need to change. For instance, you think or you have been told you are too headstrong, accommodating, selfish, incapable, and so on.

Ask yourself if the trait is a reflection of the real you. Have you been programmed by parents, guardians, social norms, or other authority figures to believe that this aspect of yourself is unacceptable? Is it true? Is it something you want to change? Do you need to? Do you hide this part of yourself behind the façade of your inner critic, martyr, self-saboteur, tough-gal, or some other inner persona? Allow yourself to give full voice to these inner aspects of you.

Once you have completed your list, have your higher-self (your inner wise woman) write you a letter from the heart. One that mirrors the truth and shines with compassion, forgiveness, acceptance, and unconditional love for yourself. Afterwards, look yourself in the eyes in a mirror. Put your hands on your heart and say out loud, "I love you." Practice this daily for a month. Notice the difference in how you feel.

Of course nobody acts out of her higher-self (inner wise woman) all the time, but it does get easier with practice. Start by observing your internal dialogues in challenging situations. Who's doing the talking? Everyone has a mob. They are the inner voices that often compete with the heart of their inner wise woman. Make a practice of becoming aware of when you are listening to the mob and how your small-self emerges. In what situations? With which people? How does your small-self get triggered? Just begin to notice. Then slowly you can begin to change your actions, despite the loud voices of your inner mob.

Wise Woman at Work

When you work out of the heart of your inner wise woman, you will shift how you make decisions and how you take action in the face of challenges. You will begin to tap into your capacity for love, compassion, gratitude, and forgiveness in all situations – whether they be hiring, firing, communicating, planning, or working with an important customer.

You make all kinds of business decisions daily. Some are more routine, and others take a bit more consideration. Routine decisions, while seemingly easy, can become so...well, routine that you may forget to consider your inner Source of knowing. It is often the small, daily decisions and actions that become the map for your bigger business landscape.

If you have a problem that keeps cropping up, you may need to review things from a different perspective. Have you gotten the team members closest to the problem involved in the solution? While this can be more time-consuming up front, it can ultimately change the landscape for the better.

For example, years ago I was an administrator in skilled nursing facilities, some of which were unionized. Scheduling certified nursing assistants (CNAs) was a royal pain in the keister! Frequently the unionized CNAs had issues with the equality and fairness of the schedule that nursing management posted.

It was frustrating to everyone, and there didn't seem to be a way to solve the problem. It became a point of contention, resulting in poor productivity, increased absenteeism, and other counterproductive work behaviors. Finally, the Director of Nursing and myself held a staff meeting. During the meeting, it was suggested that we recruit a CNA to do the scheduling. We knew just the person. She was someone that both the unionized members and management could support.

While scheduling CNAs was still a challenge, there was a lot less complaining and a huge boost in morale. Why? Because the leadership was placed in the hands of a team member who knew their teammates, their personalities, their personal issues, and the job requirements. She was better able to navigate and negotiate the needs required to schedule more effectively.

My boss was not pleased! He thought I had just invited the fox into the hen house. Management and unions are not supposed to be collaborators, in his rule book. However, using heart wisdom and discarding conventional knowledge, we were able to make the best decision for all involved.

Where are you having repeated problems? Do you need to look through your wise woman eyes to see the heart of the problem? Through the lens of the heart, you will find the courage, compassion, and love to do the things you need to.

For instance, do you need let go of a team member that never was a good fit to begin with? Why do you continue to hold on to them? Do you feel sorry for them? Are you afraid you can't replace them?

Ask yourself, what is the highest good for that person, yourself, your business, the other team members, and your customers? You may be sabotaging the success of others on the team and that of your business by hanging on to someone who needs to move on. You may actually be preventing that team member from doing some much-needed personal growth and the soul work to find their heart's path.

Whether you have a big or small decision to make, basing your decisions in heart wisdom will force the voices of the inner mob to take a back seat. That doesn't mean the Mob won't try to be backseat drivers. Most likely they will be there in the background, giving you their opinions, trying to trick you or scare you into their way of thinking. Thank them for their input and then dip into your inner wise woman. Observe and listen. She will offer you emotionally neutral, heart-centered wisdom. It still may be uncomfortable to carry out your decision, but you will because you will *know* in your heart you are making the best decision.

Especially in the midst of obstacles, strife and hardship it is easy to get disconnected from your heart-center. Your inner mob will try to get you to see yourself, your business, and others through the lens of the small-self (the glass half-empty).

To keep you centered in your heart-wisdom, it is helpful to focus on the small, joyful things in your business. Make a list of all the things, large and small, for which you are grateful. For example, I am grateful for my hot coffee in the morning, my wonderful customers, my short commute, my business partners, and so on.

Grateful Heart Mandala

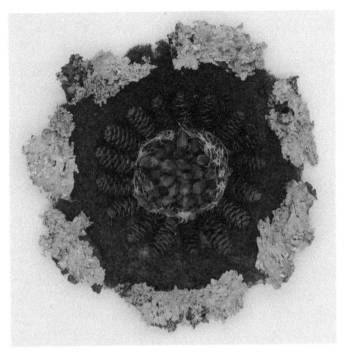

Use a template to draw a circle on a blank piece of paper or cardboard. A paper plate, pie tin, or pizza stone will do nicely, depending on how big you want your circle. Cut out the paper circle with scissors or a utility knife if using cardboard. Fill the circle with a green color using a pen, pencil, paint, or marker. This represents your fourth chakra. Draw, paint, or glue images and symbols within the circle of the things, people, or situations that you are grateful for.

You may wish to use pictures from magazines or found objects from nature or other sources such as leaves, feathers, seeds, buttons, ribbon, glitter, etc. Use one or more colors. The cardboard works best if you plan on gluing heavier objects on your mandala. Let go of the VOJ (Voice of Judgment) and allow yourself free rein. This is not supposed to be a great work of art, just an honest representation of what you are grateful for in your business at this time.

Once you are done, write about your mandala in the Notes section of this chapter. Allow yourself the freedom to write whatever comes to you. Write faster than you can think. Let your hand write the words, instead of your conscious mind. Pay no attention to grammar, punctuation, or spelling, and don't worry about whether it makes sense or not. Continue writing about your drawing until you feel you have said what you need to. Then review what you have written. Where do you see that negative thinking has gotten in the way of connecting with heartfelt gratitude?

To connect more fully with your heart-wisdom, write a gratitude list once a day for the next three weeks, and notice how your perspective on difficult issues shifts.

Your Quantum Heart

At a deeper level, we all know that the heart is vital to our well-being. It affects us and those around us energetically, emotionally, and spiritually. Think about the all the sayings that we associate with the heart – *she wears her heart on her sleeve, sick at heart, heartbroken, heartfelt, at the heart of the matter, a change of heart, follow your heart, a hardened heart, take heart, eat your heart out* – and so on. We often express our courage, love, and insight through our hearts.

Research now bears out what the sages have known for a millennium, that your heart has its own intuition, courage, and intelligence. It can affect your clarity of mind, your emotional state, your sense of spiritual connection, and ultimately your effectiveness in your business.

Your heart has its own "brain" that initiates communication with the cognitive brain through hormones, the nervous system, and biochemical and energetic pathways. Scientists have determined that the heart is a sophisticated sensory organ that emits electromagnetic energy 60 times greater than the cognitive brain, as measured by an ECG. Indeed, your heart's magnetic field is 5,000 times stronger than that of your cognitive brain. It emanates enormous energy that links you to other people and situations in ways of which you may not even be aware.

This is the idea behind the quantum heart. Remember that, according to quantum physics, everything is energy – you, your thoughts, your business, and your heart. And, since everyone and everything exchanges energy all the time, with the strength of the heart's electromagnetic energy, you have your own personal super power of attraction.

Sit up straight, put your shoulders back, and breathe deeply. Feel your chest cavity enlarge. Feel your lungs expand. Notice how it feels like your heart swells. Now release your breath. Does your chest feel lighter? Do you feel like you have more room inside your body and your mind? Do you have more clarity? Perhaps you even feel a touch happier. You have just physically experienced one of the most amazing aspects of the heart chakra – expansion!

A balanced heart chakra will help you become more expansive in multiple ways. For starters, your heart can be one of the most powerful magnetic forces of attraction in your business and your life. It expands your capacity for forgiveness, compassion, gratitude, and synchronicity, and it increases your connection with all things, living and non-living.

When you seek out positive experiences through your heart center, you evoke the law of attraction, which essentially states that you attract everything that comes into your life, both positive and negative. When you unite your thoughts with an open heart, you will attract synchronicity in the form of your highest ideals, desires, positive feelings, right actions, and love. You will find that the right situations and people come into your life and business at just the right time.

Have you ever received a phone call from someone you were thinking about, for whom you care deeply? When you answer the phone, you might say, "I was just thinking about you." This is synchronicity at work. Energetically, you vibrate with the heartfelt desire to connect with your friend or family member, and in that instant a call is set in motion.

An expansive heart is essential to synchronicity. Your heart chakra may be expansive or contracted or move from one state to the other depending on the circumstances. When expansive, you are open to giving and receiving from a place of love, joy, and gratitude. When contracted, you may not feel like giving at all or may give grudgingly, out of duty or with an ulterior motive. When working from expansiveness, you work in concert with the universal energy to attract the people and situations that are for your highest good, the highest good of your business, and the highest good of all.

How can you bring synchronicity into your business? How can you manifest your heartfelt desires? Remember the foundational structures, vision statement, mission statement, core values, and goals from the previous chapters? They are key to your success. They keep you focused on your priorities. That is why it is so important that those previous steps are centered in your heart energy.

That said, it is not uncommon to lose sight of your heart desires by getting lost in the fear of the lions and tigers and bears in the forest or by falling asleep in the field of poppies. A daily practice of breathing meditation and setting intentions will help keep you centered and walking forward on your path. Here are a couple of tools I use.

Air Your Concerns

The lungs are part of the fourth chakra, both energetically and physically. Air is the fourth chakra element. No wonder breathing is essential to our well-being. Take a moment and just notice how you breathe. Notice how your chest feels. Don't change anything you normally do, just observe. If you are like me, you may find you take shallow breaths, and your chest feels tight, especially when stressed.

When I notice myself doing this, I make sure I take several deep breaths in through my nose and out through my mouth. This does a few things. First, it brings oxygen to my brain and body and helps me relax. Second, it reduces the stress signals to my brain and gives my adrenal glands a break from producing the fight-or-flight hormone, cortisol. When overused, cortisol has been associated with fatigue and other health issues.

As a daily practice, I do a breathing mediation (well, most days). A breathing meditation is simple, while not always easy. When I sit down to meditate, I often hear an inner voice say, "I can't meditate today." I may start replaying a conversation in my mind, or my mind wanders to my "to do" list. Just to be clear, everyone's mind wanders! If you listen to some of the most well-known meditation teachers, like Tara Brach and Jack Kornfield, they will tell you their minds wander too. That is the way the brain is wired.

The key is to keep refocusing your mind on your breathing, whenever you noticed it has wandered. This may be a hundred times in two minutes. Just don't give up. Eventually you will become more focused. And then there are just those days when I seem to have no control over my mind at all. Those are the days I need my breathing meditation the most.

By focusing the mind over and over, it helps clear the clutter. You know what I'm talking about – the mind chatter that erupts when you are trying to make an important decision. Or the brain fog that sets in when you have a deadline to meet. Or the fatigue that overwhelms you just when you need that boost of energy during the second half of the week.

During moments like these, it is especially important to air your concerns. In other words, breathe air into your situation and consciously release the concern, fatigue, fear, and so on by refocusing your mind on your breathing (your air).

A Breathing Meditation Technique

Here is one breathing mediation technique. You may want to record it and play it back to yourself to help you remain focused on the process.

- Set a timer with a quiet, pleasurable alarm for 10 or more minutes. A jarring alarm is not a happy ending to a calming practice.
- Sit in a comfortable position with your eyes closed.
- Notice any tension in your body. Imagine breathing into those places individually and releasing the tension with your exhalation.
- After releasing some of your tension, continue breathing normally. No need to change how you breathe. This is about observing and allowing your breath to flow.
- Notice your breath as it enters your body. Where do you feel it? Perhaps, you feel a cool sensation at your nostrils or the back of your throat. Maybe you notice your breath as it expands your chest or your abdomen. Just notice how and where you feel it.
- Observe your breath and notice the flow of air as it enters and leaves your body. Pay attention to the split-second after the breath and before the next inhalation.
- After a few breaths, you may become aware that your mind has wandered. You may be thinking, imagining, feeling, or being distracted by noise.
- Just gently bring your awareness back to your breathing. No need to judge yourself. This is a practice, not an exercise in perfection.
- Every time your mind wanders, gently bring your focus back to your breathing. Focus on the place in your body you most feel your breath – your nostrils, throat, chest, abdomen, or perhaps some other area of your body.
- It takes a young child many attempts to master walking, and typically she will fall. In your breathing meditation, be your own calm parent encouraging your inner child to focus on your breathing, over and over and over.
- Don't worry if you find your mind wandering one time or a thousand times. Continue to bring your awareness back to your breathing.
- When the alarm sounds, allow yourself to slowly return to the present moment.

Over time, you will see a difference in your ability to increasingly maintain your focus on your breath and on the important aspects of business. As you do, you may begin to notice that you are attracting even more synchronicity. You will also find you have the clarity to know how to use it to benefit you and others in your organization.

Manifesting Your Heart's Desire

Another practice I use to attract my heart's desires is to get visual. A Manifestation Board is a great way to do this. I use the term Manifestation Board rather than vision board because the things on my board are things I intend to take action on to manifest them. If you have made a vision board, great! Now let's put some teeth into it and turn it into a Manifestation Board. (While I've done numerous vision boards over the years, I've more recently learned a technique that is more intentional.) Here is the process.[ii]

1. Get one 22- x 24-inch poster board of a color of your choice.

2. Draw lines on your poster board and segment it into six equal parts – 11 x 9.25 inches each. You can use masking tape, duct tape, glue, down ribbon or any other material to cover the lines if you would like more distinguishable borders. (There is some really fun duct tape available at many stores.)

3. Review your vision, mission, and core values statements. Also, look at your SMART goals.

4. Determine the top six priorities you want to manifest in your business at this time, and prioritize them. Write them down somewhere for future reference – perhaps on the back of your poster board, in a journal, on your goals sheet, or on a separate piece of paper.

5. Find images and words that represent your six priorities. You can look in magazines, find old pictures you may have on your computer or phone, or Google pictures and words. The main thing is that you want to be able to easily cut out or print the images and words you find.

6. Assign each section of your board one of your six priorities. Glue your images and/or words into the Manifestation Board's relevant sections. (You may have multiple images and/or words to glue into each of your six sections, or just one. There is no right way to do it. It's whatever you prefer.)

7. I recommend you use rubber cement to glue down your pictures and words. Apply it around the perimeter of each piece, so it can easily be removed. This will be important later.

8. Very important! Once complete, hang your Manifestation Board

where it is visible to you daily!

9. Spend time reviewing your Manifestation Board at least twice a day. I have a picture of mine as wallpaper on my smart phone, so I can reference it throughout the day. I also get the subliminal benefit of seeing it every time I'm on my phone.

10. Create three to five related affirmations and say them daily while reviewing your Manifestation Board.

11. Once you manifest one of your goals, remove the pictures and words from your Manifestation Board and place them in an Evidence Notebook.

12. An Evidence Notebook is a loose-leaf binder filled with clear plastic sleeves that you slip your pictures and words into. Do this for each and every accomplishment, using one sleeve per accomplishment.

13. Finally, determine what your next heart-centered goal is. Find pictures and/or words and place them in the now-empty space on your Manifestation Board.

You are creating a new habit through this process. You are reprograming your brain to align with your heart's desires. You are also aligning your energy with the greater potential of the universal energy. You are sending an energetic message to your Higher Power, guides, angels, and so on: "Hey, this is what I'm working on. Please help."

I believe that we all have powerful allies ready and willing to help. Some are earth angels, and others exist on a different universal plane. All we have to do is ask. I might add that it is tremendously helpful to them if we are clear about what we want. Your Manifestation Board shows the way.

Because your board is tied directly to your vision, mission, core values, and goals, you will be benchmarking your progress along the way through the action steps you are documenting on your goal's Tracking Form. The Tracking Form can be found in the appendixes.

You are also tracking your progress through your Evidence Notebook. This is a great way to remind yourself of your progress, especially on those days you are feeling defeated. You may even consider finding some pictures or words to put in your Evidence Notebook from previous successes, just to confirm that you are already on your heart-centered path.

A Jaded Heart

By the way, are you on your heart-centered business path? As the leader, if your heart is not in it, your business will suffer. If you hire employees whose hearts are not in it, your business will suffer. For example, several years before the writing of this book, I was involved in opening and running a small local food and crafts store as part of a traditional trades and skills school in my tiny town.

My business partners and I never intended it to become a food store at all. We started with the notion that the store would carry a few local crafts and items associated with the school. However, townspeople kept asking if we would carry more and more local food items, so we complied, even though we knew next to nothing about running a food store. Ultimately, we became a local version of a healthy convenience store. Sorry, folks, no lottery tickets or cigarettes. But local veggies, meat, snacks, beer, and wine – yes, indeed!

While it was a benefit to the community, the location wasn't ideal. We worked hard to figure out how to run it, and we hired some part-time help, one of whom was quite engaged in the local organic food market. The others were marginally engaged. All of them were bright and capable.

As owners, we argued about how it should be run, what hours it should be open, who should do what, and what we should pay employees. It took an inordinate amount of time, energy, and money. But the larger problem was that none of the three partners really wanted it in the first place. Our hearts weren't in it. In essence, each of us had a *jaded* heart when it came to this part of the business. In the Merriam-Webster dictionary, jaded is defined as "made dull, apathetic, or cynical." And we were all of those.

It's hard to spark enthusiasm in your team with jaded leadership. As you might guess, the store did not thrive. After a few years, we closed it due to poor profitability. In retrospect, we should have stayed within our mission and our heart's desires. No doubt, we would have had more energy to do the things that were really important to us and our business, and we would have had a lot more money at the end of the day.

I find it interesting that the stone for the fourth chakra is green jade. Green jade is known for its ability to help heal the fourth chakra and for its healing properties in general. A partial list of other aspects green jade supports includes calmness, tranquility, longevity, protection, meditation, wisdom, prosperity, luck, problem-solving, and strength.

The color green is also associated with prosperity, success, and money. (*Just show me the green!*) In addition, it represents spring and new beginnings. It is the most predominant color on earth. Green leafy vegetables (especially kale) are considered a superfood. In general, leafy greens are some of the most nutritious foods we can eat and have many healing properties.

The energetic healing properties of the color green and the jade stone can be used to heal your jaded heart and help direct your heart energy into projects that really matter to you and your business.

I certainly had to do some healing of my own jaded heart after we closed our local food convenience store. By focusing on my heart chakra, I did some much-needed forgiving of those I blamed for getting us into the financial situation to begin with (myself included). I received forgiveness from those individuals who were negatively impacted by the closing. And I reconnected with my gratitude for the new opportunities that presented themselves just when that chapter of my life ended.

What about you? What is the quality of your heart energy in your business? Write about the quality of both your heart energy and the heart energy of other stakeholders in the Notes section of this chapter. Do you feel like you put your whole heart into your business? I'm not talking about workaholism. I'm interested in how you energetically connect your heart to your business.

In the Notes Section of this chapter, also write the answers to the following questions:

1. Do you approach your business from a place of excitement, positive intentions, and a sunny outlook, or is your point of view negative, worried, and uncertain?

2. What about others in your business? Do their attitudes and actions bring about positive outcomes?

3. If you were able to measure your organizational electromagnetic heart energy, how would it rate – high, medium, or low?

4. Are there areas where you need to heal your jaded heart? What are they?

5. How will you go about healing?

Putting Heart and Soul in the Bottom Line

Putting your money to work in positive ways is another way to set your business on a heart-centered path. As a leader, you have to balance matters of the heart with the higher good of the organization. On a practical level, you have to balance taking care of your team while maintaining the profitability of your business. You have to balance the need for excellent quality with the understanding that to err is human. There is also the delicate balance of being grateful for the progress you are making on your goals while still expecting more. And, of course, you have to balance meaningful relationships while taking care of business. These feats might leave you feeling like you are walking on a tightrope without a safety net!

People are at the heart of every business. Their innovation, heartfelt hard work, attitudes, and energy are central to any thriving organization. And yet, employees don't always get treated with the love and respect they deserve. In some organizations, people are little more than a resource, just like money is a resource, except money often gets treated with more respect.

Is it possible to embrace the human spirit and the bottom line? I say it definitely is! The heart chakra is smack-dab in the middle of the seven chakras. It is the energetic balancing point. As such, it reminds us to also create balance in the workplace from a heart-centered place.

Money is a first chakra issue, and the financial safety and security of your business need to be balanced with the wisdom of the heart chakra. When it comes to money, you are at a disadvantage culturally. Money (and what it can buy) has become one of the most important symbols of power and success, eclipsing a more heart-centered approach to business. At times, there may be pressure to focus on money over relationships. Most people have been programed since they were children to believe there is never enough money to go around. This may lead you to be driven by fear of scarcity rather than by choices that reflect your vision, mission, and core values.

Do you allow money to define you and your business, or do you use money to further your vision, mission, and core values? Giving and receiving money from a heart-centered place is more important to a successful business than just accumulating it for the sake of the bottom line. Don't get me wrong, money is a wonderful thing. I like money – a lot! That said, money is energy, just like everything else. As energy, money is meant to be exchanged. Pure accumulation, at the expense of balanced, life-affirming spending and responsible future planning, shuts down the exchange. When that exchange shuts down, so does the good that money can do in your business and the world. Have you ever made business decisions based on chasing money, rather than based in the wisdom of your heart center? I know I have, and it usually doesn't work out well in the long run.

When your focus on the bottom line supersedes the needs of the people in your business, you create a low energetic vibration. This may turn up as low morale and unproductive work behaviors, like absenteeism or increased errors. You will not attract the quality of people you desire. To increase the flow of money, invest money, time, and actions into long-range positive outcomes, rather than short-term profits. You will set the tone for more of the same to come into your business.

By investing in paying the best wage and benefits package possible, developing caring team relationships, and providing growth opportunities, you will attract quality people. Your organization will build a positive culture based on these energetic investments. In turn, your business will reap the profits financially, as well as connecting future synchronistic heart-centered benefits to you, your employees, customers, other stakeholders, and the larger community.

There are companies that bank on doing business where value is placed on people first. One of those is Rackspace, a computer technology company that manages cloud service. Their core values include fanatical customer support in all they do. They also require results first (substance over flash). Rackers (a term used for team members) are like friends and family, and they have passion for their work. Rackspace believes in full disclosure and transparency, and they are committed to greatness. Incidentally, they are great believers in giving back to their community as well.[iii]

Not surprisingly, Rackspace is doing very well financially. They attract high-quality people to work in their organization, and they've created a culture that celebrates the human spirit and profitability.[iv] They know how to put heart and soul in the bottom line.

In the Notes section of this chapter, answer the following questions:

1. Do your business core values balance the human spirit with the bottom line?

2. Do your business practices reflect the heart and soul of money?

3. How is money reinvested in the people working at your organization? In the community? In the greater world?

4. Do you feel there needs to be a shift in the energy of money in your business? In what way?

5. How might you go about this?

Putting It Into Practice

At Rainbow Integrated Health's quarterly board meeting, Megan speaks from her heart about her observations and concerns as a naturopathic doctor and a team member at RIH. Red in the face and with teeth clenched, Valerie is visibly angered by Megan's remarks. She feels the comments are personally directed at her. She retaliates by announcing loudly that Megan, and indeed most of the members of the team, have been shirking their duties. She continues with a laundry list of recent incidents: gossiping in the halls, calling out sick, failure to follow her directives, making too many mistakes, etc. Valerie then states that she thinks it's time to clean house. Tomorrow she will initiate individual conferences with team members and issue written warnings to those at fault.

Board members and RIH team members are stunned into silence. On the surface, Valerie's remarks mirror recent behaviors. Yet, they don't reflect what is going on at a deeper organizational level.

Susan, the board chair, is the first to speak. She is well-versed in organizational behaviors and knows that some vital information is missing. She moves that she and members of the board conduct private, individual interviews with the RIH team members prior to issuing any written reprimands. Board members agree unanimously. She quickly assigns board members to individual team members. She opts to speak privately with Valerie herself.

The courage required for Megan to speak up in the face of Valerie's potential wrath comes from her heart center. When initially listening to her inner mob, her small-self was immobilized in fear and failed to take action. But later, she gets in touch with her inner wise woman. She knows in her heart that, for the higher good of everyone, she must speak up, even if it means the loss of her job. There is too much at stake. Not only is there the potential loss of the other practitioners on the team, but the quality of patient care is at risk. In the end, the larger mission and goals of RIH will fail to be realized.

Valerie, on the other hand, continues to listen to her inner mob. Her small-self reacts from a wounded heart. She hides her own feelings of disempowerment behind her inner bully, who has a strong need to exert power and control over others. She has yet to learn how to tap into the wisdom of her heart center.

Susan is a wise woman, who internally acknowledges her small-self's emotional reaction to the situation and is able to set it aside and tune in to her neutral observer. She leans into her heart-centered intelligence to make the decision to meet with individual team members.

Taking Action

Now it's time for you to take action. Carry out the following activities to help you determine what your next steps need to be in order to be able to appropriately harness and exercise the fourth chakra power of your business.

1. Take the Chakra Assessment that follows and record your score. Does it indicate a glaring deficit in this chakra or just some tweaking?

2. Answer the Questions for Further Exploration that follow and write down any insights, new ideas, or awareness you may have.

3. Listen to the Heart of Quan Yin guided journey on the website and journal about your experience: www.nanettegiacoma.com/OpenForBusinessBook.

4. Review the information and insights you have gathered from this chapter about the fourth chakra.

5. Read Ways to Balance Your fourth Chakra, which follows, and select which things you want to try, or make your own list of ideas.

6. From your list, choose 1-3 things you are going to do.

    a.___ What action steps will you take?

    b.___ Do you need help? What kind of help? From whom?

    c.___ When will you start? What is your goal completion date?

    d.___ How will you know you have reached your goal?

FOURTH CHAKRA ASSESSMENT

Fourth Chakra	Yes	No	Somewhat
Do you have primarily positive thoughts and emotions about your business?			

Do you follow your heart when making difficult decisions?			
Is there an attitude of gratitude about work in your business?			
Do you have a way for team members to give back to the community?			
Are work relationships with team members and other stakeholders loving and caring?			
Do you and team members have a deep sense of unity and connection with each other? With stakeholders? With the greater community?			
In difficult situations, is judgment suspended in favor of compassion and understanding?			
Do you feel there is "heart" in your bottom line?			
Do you take advantage of synchronicity on your business path?			
Do you attract the people, things, and situations you want in your business?			
Do you and team members see each other as equals?			

Do you and others in your business mostly forgive mistakes?			
SCORE			

Give yourself 2 points for every Yes, 1 point for every Somewhat, and 0 points for No.

Scale: 4-12 points: Strong need for fourth chakra balancing

13-20 points: Some fourth chakra balancing needed

21-28 points: Congratulations! The fourth chakra of your business is well-balanced.

Questions for Further Exploration

1. Describe your emotional work environment. How do you or team members create a caring, supportive work environment with each other, customers, and other stakeholders?

2. Is there a code of secrecy that includes some and excludes others at work? (Not to be confused with confidentiality.) Why? What kind of dynamics does it create?

3. Where is there excessive finger-pointing and/or judgment of others? What kinds of behaviors are exhibited when this goes on? Why do you think that is?

4. Where and how can you spark more of an "attitude of gratitude" among team members?

5. Where are there general feelings of lack? How is this demonstrated?

6. How do you wish to incorporate a system for team members to give back to the community in which you work/live? If you have one, what is it and how is it being utilized?

7. How do your and/or others' moods direct the day's emotional pulse? How does the prevalent mood affect the workflow and attitudes of others?

8. Describe your personal interactions with team members and customers. Is there ever any tendency to push team members, customers, or other stakeholders away? Why?

9. What are the prevalent thoughts and emotions (positive and/or negative) regarding work? Give some examples of how this has

attracted more of the same.

10. Give some examples of how you have taken advantage of synchronicity in your business.

Ways to Balance Your Fourth Chakra
ᑡᴄᑭ Business

- ❑ Schedule times for team members to gather outside of work to connect socially.
- ❑ Become a learning organization where mistakes are used as educational tools for personal development and business growth.
- ❑ Implement a reward system for solutions for ongoing issues, using recognition, financial rewards, or incentives (for example, paid time off).
- ❑ Do a team-building retreat.
- ❑ Hold a community event or host a fundraising event.
- ❑ Create a schedule of company giving where you and team members give time or money to a nonprofit cause.
- ❑ Create a company Manifestation Board.
- ❑ Place an interactive company Gratitude Board in a common area.
- ❑ Bring live green plants into workspaces and common areas and/or landscape around the building or office.
- ❑ Install full-spectrum lighting in work areas.
- ❑ Put air purifiers in workspaces for air that is fresh, clean, and free of toxins.
- ❑ Give breathing breaks throughout the day to team members.
- ❑ Lead a ten-minute morning breathing meditation that's open to all team members.
- ❑ Find a green smoothie recipe of the week and share with team members.

ᑡᴄᑭ Body

- ❑ Eat fourth chakra foods. Think green! Eat more green vegetables and fruit or drink green smoothies.
- ❑ Drink hot tea or water.
- ❑ Do deep breathing exercises several times a day.

- ❑ Get fresh air by taking walks in nature.
- ❑ When seasonally viable, open windows in your home and office.
- ❑ Do Bhakti yoga.
- ❑ Do regular cardiovascular exercise like jogging, biking, or an elliptical machine.
- ❑ Uncross your legs while sitting.
- ❑ Take stretch breaks every couple of hours while at work.
- ❑ Take a hot bath.
- ❑ Diffuse or wear the following essential oils. For the lungs: cinnamon, respiratory blend, frankincense, or peppermint. For the heart and circulation: ginger, lavender, peppermint, wild orange, or ylang-ylang.

ᏯᎦ Emotions

- ❑ Say, "I'm sorry" when you make mistakes.
- ❑ Get a pet.
- ❑ Create a daily forgiveness practice:
  - Say out loud, "I forgive (fill in the name)."
  - Ask for forgiveness out loud: "Please forgive me, (fill in the name)."
- ❑ Practice kindness, tolerance, and acceptance with others every day.
- ❑ Give and get four hugs daily.
- ❑ Laugh! Watch comedies or engage in humorous events.
- ❑ Do daily mindful breathing meditations.
- ❑ Make a list of people that you love or have loved in your life.
- ❑ Practice being aware of your harsh judgements of yourself and others and send love and compassion in those moments.
- ❑ Look yourself in the eyes in the mirror. Put your hands on your heart and say out loud, "I love you." Notice how you feel.
- ❑ Diffuse or wear the following essential oils: rose, geranium, wild orange, or renewing blend.

ᏯᎦ Energy

- ❑ Wear jewelry with or carry green jade, emerald, or rose quartz.

❑ Create a spiritual family of friends or colleagues.

❑ Create a garden at home.

❑ Wear green clothing.

❑ Say "I'm sorry" when you make mistakes.

❑ Create a list of the people and things you are grateful for in your business.

❑ Create a personal Manifestation Board.

❑ Tell team members and customers how much you appreciate them.

❑ Write down ten things you are grateful for every day for three weeks.

❑ List old hurts, negative attitudes, and paradigms you need to release, and then burn the list.

❑ Avoid spending time with negative people.

❑ Avoid listening to or watching negative programs.

❑ Diffuse or wear the following essential oils: grounding blend, geranium, rose, or ylang-ylang.

∽ Affirmations for the Fourth Chakra

❑ I love myself fully.

❑ I love others unconditionally.

❑ I am compassionate.

❑ I forgive easily.

❑ I am joyful.

❑ I easily release past hurts.

❑ I am grateful for my business.

❑ I am grateful for the people in my business.

❑ I attract only people, things, and situations for my highest good.

❑ I easily balance giving and receiving.

Guided Journey: The Heart of Quan Yin

Imagine you are in the middle of a sea of green, green grass; it whorls around you, enveloping you in warm lushness. This is the Meadow of Mercy and Compassion. Here you can open up and heal your wounds of the heart, forgive deeply, feel great gratitude, and experience profound love. The sun shines brightly in a clear blue sky. A meadowlark sings in the tall grass, unseen. It seems it is singing just to you. Listen to its flute-like song. As it sings, you feel the song in your heart. Mesmerized, you follow the spellbinding song. As you seek the meadowlark, you weave through the tall, gorgeous grass, with no need for directions.

After what seems like a long time, you realize you no longer hear the song of the meadowlark and find you are standing at the edge of an emerald pool surrounded by soft, spongy moss. At the center is the meadowlark, perched on a stalk of beautiful bamboo located on a tiny, tiny island. This is the Island of Love and Harmony. The bamboo begins to sway, keeping a rhythmic beat in the wind…chhh, chhh, chhh. The meadowlark flies away. As it does, the bamboo appears to grow taller and taller, creating a shady canopy of green and gold.

Beneath the canopy stands Quan Yin, the Chinese goddess of mercy and compassion. She hears the cries of all beings. Her name literally means "the one who hears the sounds of the world." What does she look like? Feel her divine love and abundant kindness emanating to you and out into the world. She asks you to walk to the island through the shallow, emerald water. As you step into the water, you feel a tingle of energy rise from the bottom of your feet, up through your legs, your hips, your torso, until the energy reaches your heart.

Walk slowly and deliberately to stand before her. Gaze deeply into her eyes. Feel her strength and compassion for you. She knows all your wounds, your addictions, your anger, your disappointments, and your sadness. And your love, your gratitude, your compassion, and your heart's desires. There is no judgment. Notice everything you can about this moment.

On this Island of Love and Harmony, you can ask Quan Yin for whatever you need to heal your wounded heart, and it will be granted. Ask for healing now. Quan Yin whispers to you what you need to do to balance your heart chakra. Listen carefully. What does she tell you?

She hands you a piece of green jade. Hold it to your heart. Feel the green healing warmth enter your heart and travel throughout your entire body. It completely embraces you in its healing power. The energy then expands to encompass your life, your business, and the world at large. Continue receiving this energy until all aspects of your body, mind, and soul are enveloped in green healing light. Look at the jade stone. It is illuminated, with a symbol of balance carved into it. What symbol do you hold? Carry this symbol in your heart from now on.

As you focus on the symbol, the landscape around you becomes a glittery, green haze. It sparkles into every cell of your being. Feel the expansiveness in your heart. Quan Yin smiles and embraces you deeply. You melt into her divine love. In this moment, know Quan Yin is always with you, no matter where you are. Pause and fully appreciate her gift. Still holding divine love in your heart, start to bring your attention back into the room, and when you hear the chimes, you will return to ordinary reality.

 **Notes**

❧ **Notes** ❧

❧ CHAPTER 7 ❧

Fifth Chakra: True Blue Communication

The conversation is the relationship.

Susan Scott

Daring greatly means the courage to be vulnerable.
To ask for what you need.
To talk about how you're feeling.
To have the hard conversations.

Brené Brown

CHAKRA 5 QUICK REFERENCE GUIDE

FIFTH CHAKRA	CORRELATIONS
Sanskrit Name	Visuddha
Meaning	Purification
Location	Throat
In the Body Governs	Throat, thyroid, esophagus, trachea, neck, mouth, ears, teeth
Endocrine Gland	Thyroid
Imbalances	Sore throats, thyroid issues, toxicity, stiff shoulders, tight neck, hearing loss, or speech difficulties; don't speak up about what you are feeling, don't speak your mind, build walls around yourself from others; anxiety, secrecy, frustration; it is the voice of the wounded inner child that may lash out or yell; nonstop talking or not listening; blocked creativity
Energetic Goals	Authentic self-expression, harmony with others, creativity, good communication, and resonance with yourself and others; fulfilled destiny
Rights	To speak
Color	Bright sky blue
Food	Liquids in general, water, fruit juices, herbal teas, soups; seaweeds, like kelp or kombu, contain iodine to support thyroid function; tart or tangy fruits – lemons, limes, grapefruit, kiwi; also bluish/reddish fruit – blueberries, blackberries, grapes, and cherries

Element	Ether, sound
Stones	Turquoise
Animal	White elephant, bull, sparrow hawk
Archetype	Hermes – Greek god of travelers, thieves, and messenger of the gods. Iris – Greek goddess of the rainbow and messenger of the gods. Sarasvati – Hindu goddess of learning, wisdom, and communication
Plant	Gardenia
Music	Musical note G
Essential Oil	Ylang-ylang, lavender, chamomile, gardenia

Communication on all levels is one of the primary energetic goals of the fifth chakra. The god Hermes and the goddess Iris, as messengers of the Greek gods, were ancient communication specialists of sorts. They had to have the skills, aptitude, and resources to effectively interact with all kinds of clients, team members, and other stakeholders – not only gods and goddesses, but mortals and other legendary creatures as well, perhaps a centaur or a cyclops or two.

Certainly, Hermes had an advantage with his winged athletic shoes, and Iris had a full set of rainbow-colored wings on her back. Handy when one needs to engage in face-to-face communication.

But how about you? What if you were a messenger of the gods? What skills, aptitudes, and resources would you need? How would you communicate? How would you listen? How would you speak? How would you connect the messages you give and receive to your inner wise woman, so that they are god/dess worthy?

Certainly you would want to be sure that you are listening deeply to all that is being communicated, using your physical, emotional, and intuitive senses. You would want to take into account the personality of the god or goddess with whom you are communicating. What is their speaking style, body language, unconscious blind spots, and distorting filters based upon their perceptions of reality? You would most likely approach Zeus, the god of the sky, in a different way than Poseidon, the god of the sea. How would you go about chatting with Aphrodite, the goddess of love and beauty, versus Artemis, the goddess of the moon and hunting?

If you have read any of the Greek tragedies, you know that the gods are a changeable lot. Actions were often based on their personalities and moods. It seems many of them had an attitude of "hear no evil, see no evil, speak no evil" when it came to receiving messages. They really didn't like bad news! Of course, it totally depended on that god or goddess's interpretation of evil, which varied greatly.

For instance, Hades, the god of the underworld, would be prone to killing the messenger just for the Hades of it. Hephaestus, the god of blacksmithing and fire, really doesn't like people and probably would just forge ahead, not even giving you the time of day. And Athena, the goddess of wisdom, war, and utilitarian arts, might give you one of her beautiful weavings if she liked your message. If not, she might leave you spinning a web of woe for all eternity like she did to Arachne.

Just think, if you were a messenger of the gods, you would have to climb up Mt. Olympus every day to share information that might or might not be received well. Oh, wait! You do climb communication mountains every day – at least metaphorically. And, sometimes that communication doesn't go as planned.

Hear No Evil

Do you or others in your organization hear no evil? Evil in this instance is not about morality; rather, it is about choosing not to listen to another person's point of view. You don't have to be a Greek god to filter what is being said through your personal biases and perceptions of truth and reality. We humans also do it all the time.

When someone says something you disagree with, you may consider them wrong, ignorant, annoying, etc. Even before you truly try to hear the other person's point of view, you may have your mind already made up and stop listening. At some level, they become the "evil," the "other," the one not worth hearing. In that moment, you choose to "hear no evil."

We all have biases that interfere with our ability to listen with an open heart. These are called distorting filters, and everyone has them. For instance, you may seek perfection in all you do, but the problem is that your definition of perfection is not everyone's. Or you may always worry about what others are thinking about you, so you scrutinize their words for negative connotations (real or imagined). Maybe you are a get-it-done kind of leader and have no patience for slower ways of processing information. You may see people who are "slow" to interpret what you say as a weak link.

This kind of right/wrong or us/them thinking, often leads to misunderstandings, interrupts communication flow between team members, and creates dysfunctional work relationships. It sets up communication barriers that result in fifth chakra organization-wide imbalances.

I've seen this manifest in organizations in a number of ways. It isn't uncommon for departments within an organization to stop working with each other effectively because of a communication breakdown. There may be differences of opinion about resource allocation, priorities, leadership expectations, etc., all of which end up creating conflict and a prevalent attitude of "hear no evil." Team members may waste time and energy gossiping about the other team and persuading others of their way of thinking. No one wants to listen to the opposing viewpoint.

How do you create an organization in which team members are willing to listen to alternate points of view? First, you have to make such a willingness a priority for you, and then make time to dive deep into the hard conversations that Brené Brown talks about in her book *Braving the Wilderness*. Depending on the magnitude of the problem, you may need an outside facilitator for this or you may be comfortable facilitating it yourself.

Begin by looking at your business from an eagle's-eye view. What is for the highest good of your business? (Don't forget to check in with your heart center.) Conversations need to be taken out of the realm of personalities and personal agendas.

Start with yourself. Catch yourself blocking your fifth chakra sense of hearing. Practice recognizing your biases and setting them aside to really listen to the other's point of view. That doesn't mean you will agree; it just means you are open to greater understanding. Open your listening to incorporate the compassion, love, and wisdom that are associated with your heart chakra. Set your intentions for resonance with others, which is one of the fifth chakra energetic goals.

Resonance implies vibration. When speaking, we use the vibration of our vocal cords to make words. When listening, we take in the vibration of another's words. Remember that all of this is energy! You are sending energy through the vibration of your words and receiving energy through listening. Once your words are out there, you can't take their energy back. When speaking, what kind of energy do you want to send? When listening, do you fully allow for the underlying vibrational energy to speak to you?

I'm not just talking about what words are being used. I'm also referring to the energy behind the words. Authentic communication is a choice. It can only be achieved by digging deeper than the words into the underlying truth, which can get pretty uncomfortable at times, especially because your truth will most likely be different than mine.

When looking at the truth of a communication problem in an organization, be the eagle. Soar into the ethers, above the drama, personalities, and personal agendas – all of which generally lie in the small-self. Ether is the fifth chakra element. In this case, ether refers to the air that lies above the clouds. It is the vibrational medium of light and will help you raise your vibrational energy to become more enlightened. What hard conversations do you need to have that will clear the air in your business?

In the Notes section of this chapter, write down three people in your business with whom you need to have a hard conversation. Once you have determined the three people, write the answers to the following questions in the Notes section of this chapter for each of the three individuals.

1. Name the issue in succinct terms, giving specific examples that illustrate it.

2. What do you believe is at the heart of the issue? Is it a recurring problem or something that seemingly suddenly blew up in your face? Do you know the underlying reason?

3. Review the history. How did the issue start? Where? When? Why? Who was involved? What extenuating circumstances were present? Have there been other conversations and actions to try to resolve the issue?

4. Why is it important to have the hard conversation? What's at stake? How does it affect your bottom line, goals, attitudes, motivation, relationships, team effort, etc.? Be specific about the potential negative impact.

5. How have you contributed to the issue – your behaviors, actions, or inaction?

6. What would you like the outcome of the hard conversation to be? Resolution? Solution? Results? Be sure that you are open to ideas other than your own. This is not about you getting your way; this is about finding a new path forward.

You can use the above information as an outline for those hard conversations you need to have. When you open the energetic lines of communication to find the underlying truth of the issue, you will find the courage to authentically communicate. It requires vulnerability on your part, and asking for authenticity and vulnerability from others. The truth often lies beneath the words. Dip down into the emotions, the passions, the subconscious shadows, and the energy that lie at the bottom of the well and allow for open, honest communication to come to light.

See No Evil

Effective communication is a whole mind, body, and spirit experience. "See no evil" means you don't use your senses to the fullest extent to help you understand what is being communicated. You don't "see" the other person fully. What is their speaking style? What is their body language saying? What are their facial expressions? How do they seem emotionally (beneath the superficial "I'm fine")? What is their demeanor? What do you notice about their energy? What other nonverbal messages are they sending?

As a leader, you may get so caught up in conveying your message that you fail to really notice all the cues that deepen your connection with the other person. Everyone is unique, and so is their style of communicating. Take body language, for example. It is easy to observe, but not always easy to interpret. One person may have open, graceful body movements, smile often, and have a relaxed facial expression. Are they unconsciously trying to put you at ease? Or perhaps they want you to like them. Another person may appear intimidating and perfectly put together with matching clothes and shoes. They may appear confident – shoulders back, chest out, a wide stance. Whether they truly are confident is another matter. Still another may appear aloof, self-contained, with unanimated body language and few facial expressions.

How might you experience each of these people? How would you approach your communication with them? It's important to remember that communication styles are typically not about you! How often do you take body language personally? I know I do, usually when my small-self is active, and I'm communicating from my own biases and blind spots. It is key to stay centered in your wise woman when observing speaking styles, facial expressions, body language, and other nonverbal communication. Most is unconscious on the other person's part. It is often an outer expression of subconscious conversations with their inner mob.

Body language and other nonverbal communication can be rich sources of information when approached from a place of curiosity. By that I mean don't assume that you know what the other person is thinking based on nonverbal cues. You know what they say about ass-u-me, and it's true! Use your curiosity to ask questions that create clarity and be ready to uncover someone's authentic self. Not the small-self who is hiding behind the unconscious nonverbal cues, but the whole person who is energetically available to converse at a more intimate level.

Use your whole self in this process of discovery. The Buddhists have a concept called beginner's mind. In the beginner's mind, there are many possibilities. In the expert's mind, there are few. Get clear of preconceived notions that limit your thinking about what is being communicated. Instead, become curious about what is possible. Be like a child. Children ask a lot of questions, they are observant, and they are curious about almost everyone. They are looking for information, not making judgements about others. How can you as a leader bring this element to your communication with your team?

A person will know at some level whether you are genuine in your communication efforts and fully engaged. Ask questions that let them know that you are truly interested in their opinions and insights. What do you want to learn about this person? Take notes to show you are paying attention. Ask for clarification where you are fuzzy in your understanding.

Another important element of authentic communication is being truly present. A Chinese proverb says, "When a question is posed ceremoniously, the Universe responds." Think about the intent behind a ceremony. One or more people are present to participate in an important event. One of the most powerful energetic actions you can take when communicating is to be fully present in the moment. Give the person with whom you are communicating your full attention. Make it an event worth attending!

Which means that whether communicating in person, by phone, or virtually, turn off any other distractions. This may include, your cell phone, email, and facebook (unless you are using these to communicate). Turn off anything that will ding, buzz, or chime. Don't act interested; *be* interested! There is nothing more annoying and disrespectful than someone being half present during a conversation. Do you scan email when on the phone? Even on the phone, I can tell when someone is doing something else. Generally, I too will end up only partially engaged, and then what's the point? Where's the connection? There isn't one!

Every conversation you have will be building, destroying, or preserving the status quo in your relationships. Consider asking a few people you trust both personally and professionally to give you honest feedback about your communication presence, your speaking style, and other, nonverbal kinds of communication that you exhibit.

Use your Buddhist beginner's mind for this exercise. Come from a place of curiosity and learning. How do others perceive you? Where do you communicate from your small-self and your own set of unconscious nonverbal cues? How is your inner mob interfering with your authentic communication? In the Notes section of this chapter, write down what you learn.

Speak No Evil

"Speak no evil" refers to those uncomfortable topics that members of an organization don't want to bring up. Authentic self-expression, harmony with others, and good communication are major energetic goals of the fifth chakra. None of these can be achieved if people aren't speaking honestly about their thoughts and feelings.

Harmony can often be misinterpreted to mean "no disagreement", but that is not the case. Harmony can only happen when you and others speak up about essential truths, which may or may not align with each other. People often feel uncomfortable talking about the areas of disagreement in a situation or a decision, and that often contributes to and sometimes leads to incomplete organizational understanding. Subsequently, not everyone is on board when it's time to move forward with goals and actions. You may end up with other problems as well, like lack of motivation to complete a project, inter-departmental conflict, or subversive office politics.

As a leader, you may unknowingly exacerbate the issue, especially if there is uncertainty about disagreeing with leadership, or if rocking the boat is considered counterculture. Team members may be so concerned about causing overt conflict that they fail to publically speak up. Actually, too much agreement in an organization may indicate there is a greater "evil" lurking, because open, authentic communication has gone underground. Surface agreement rarely leads to the deeper commitment needed to energetically connect the organizational chakras for a successful business.

Knowing that it is safe to communicate honestly helps team members to balance first chakra needs for safety and belonging at work. Allowing for authentic feelings to be expressed engages the second chakra's need for connection and fosters passion for the organizational vision and mission. Having a say in goals and how they are accomplished connects the third chakra sense of purpose with the personal will to take action. Communicating from a heart-centered place, magnifies the fourth chakra's energy so that compassion and understanding are likely to prevail, even in the face of differences.

Close your eyes for a moment and allow a difficult work situation to come to mind. Imagine a circle of team members (yourself included) in a business meeting. All members are invited to communicate openly, honestly, authentically, and respectfully about the causes and solutions to this situation. How does balanced sharing occur? How are team members given an opportunity to truly convey their thoughts, feelings, and concerns? How are all invited to disagree? How is deep listening encouraged? How does everyone engage their creative problem-solving ability to offer up solutions? How do you and others at the meeting open up energetically to giving and receiving authentic communication?

In the Notes section of this chapter, write down what you imagined in the present tense. Write down all the details and how you feel about holding a meeting this way. Is it a positive experience in your imagination, or is it challenging? Why?

The Circle Way: A Leader in Every Chair, by Christina Baldwin and Ann Linnea, is an excellent resource for creating a structure for powerful meetings where everyone has an opportunity to lead, be present, listen deeply, share openly, develop creative solutions, and transform organizational fifth chakra energy so that authentic communication prevails. I have participated and led what Baldwin and Linnea call the PeerSpirit Circle Process. I find it to be an excellent tool to transform old habits of communication into sincere dialogues characterized by respectful and compassionate listening. I encourage you to adopt this process and use it to create more effective, meaningful meetings.

True Blue Communication Mandala

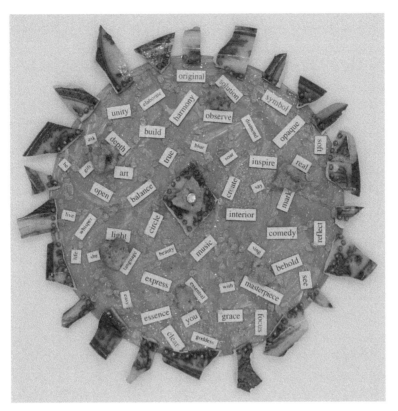

Use a template to draw a circle on a blank piece of paper or cardboard. A paper plate, pie tin, or pizza stone will do nicely, depending on how big you want your circle. Cut out the paper circle with scissors or a utility knife if using cardboard. Fill the circle with a bright blue color using a pen, pencil, paint, or marker. This represents your fifth chakra. Draw, paint, or glue images and symbols within the circle that express open, honest, authentic communication. You may wish to use pictures from magazines or found objects from nature or other sources such as leaves, feathers, seeds, buttons, ribbon, glitter, etc. Use one or more colors. The cardboard works best if you plan on gluing heavier objects on your mandala.

Let go of the VOJ (Voice of Judgment) and allow yourself free rein. This is not supposed to be a great work of art, just a sincere representation of open, honest, authentic communication.

Once you are done, write about your mandala. Allow yourself the freedom to write whatever comes to you. Write faster than you can think. Let your hand write the words, instead of your conscious mind. Pay no attention to grammar, punctuation, or spelling, and don't worry about whether it makes sense or not. Continue writing about your mandala until you feel you have said what you need to. Then review what you have written.

How open, honest, and authentic is the communication in your business? Where do you need to change the fifth chakra energy around communication? What are the outcomes of any imbalances in the organizational fifth chakra? Keep this information handy for use in the Taking Action section of this chapter.

Manifest Destiny

Communication is also vital to fulfilling your destiny in your lifetime. A fulfilled destiny is another energetic goal of the fifth chakra, and it's kind of a big deal. When you look at destiny in terms of how you communicate your soul-purpose with the larger world, it makes sense that it is included in the energy of the fifth chakra. You may change how you reach your destiny (soul-purpose) in life, but ultimately each path you walk brings you closer to it.

Consider your business as one leg of the journey on the road to your personal destiny. How do you tie your business into your soul-purpose? Do your vision and mission reflect your business destiny? Do your core values speak to your commitment to manifesting your vision and mission? Do you walk your talk with team members and customers?

I have been a part of a few organizations that had great philosophies but that didn't walk their talk. One that comes to mind had an inverted organizational chart where the employees were placed at the top and leadership at the bottom. They claimed that the employees were at the top because they were most important to the success of the organization. Absolutely true!

However, when it came to paying employees a living wage, providing decent benefits, or treating them with respect, the organizational chart went out the window. Lower to average industry standard wages and benefits prevailed throughout the organization. Top management regularly booted out quality middle managers who were outspoken. Yet the organization's leaders didn't see the disparity between their walk and talk.

How about you? What's your talk? How are you walking it? Both words and actions are necessary to fully communicate your purpose as a good business citizen. Each action you take will reflect how you are fulfilling your business destiny, how you are communicating your bigger organizational purpose.

In previous chapters, I've given you some insight into how to take action in your daily practices with yourself and your organization to walk your talk, but how about walking that talk out in the bigger world? Specifically, how are you conveying your marketing message?

Seriously? Marketing as a tool for manifesting your destiny? Yes! Because your marketing is about communicating your business message to the larger world at a deeper energetic level. What does your marketing message communicate about who you are and what you do?

Remember your third chakra core values? They are the guiding principles for your organization and are the fundamental beliefs that underpin your organizational identity. Your core values provide a guide for your marketing path. They are the heart of your marketing strategy. Your core values drive who you want to service (ideal customer), communicate your destiny/purpose/mission (branding), and help determine the road of highest good to get the word out (marketing plan).

What kind of customers are you attracting into your business? Are they who you envisioned? Are they attracted to your product and services because they support your core values? Are you authentically communicating those values through your branding? Do you have a plan in place that helps you reach your ideal customer in the best way possible?

It is very important to carry out the analytical research about customer needs, target markets, trends, etc. Research is a way of receiving communication. Research is energy in the form of information that you decide to take in (or not). There are plenty of books available that can guide you about how to do the necessary research, as well as help you create a marketing strategy and plan.

A good place to start looking at your marketing message is a SWOT analysis. SWOT stands for Strengths, Weakness, Opportunities, and Threats. Strengths and weaknesses are assets and liabilities within your business as it exists presently. Opportunities and threats refer to things external to your business that may happen in the future. In the Notes section of this chapter, brainstorm your own marketing SWOT analysis. You may wish to follow up with a brainstorming session that includes other stakeholders as well. Remember that brainstorming is about allowing the ideas, words, and energy to flow. No VOJ allowed. Brainstorm the answers to these questions in terms of your marketing message.

1. Strengths:
   - What do you do well?
   - What unique resources do you draw upon?
   - What do others see as your strengths?
2. Weaknesses:
   - Where could you improve?
   - Where do you have fewer resources?
   - What would others see as your weaknesses?
3. Opportunities:
   - What good opportunities are open to you?
   - What trends can you take advantage of?
   - Where can you turn your strengths into opportunities?
4. Threats:
   - What trends could harm you?
   - What is the current market environment for your type of business?
   - What threats could your weaknesses expose you to?

Notice if you came up with any new ideas or perspectives during your SWOT analysis, and highlight this information. Make a few notes about how you might change your marketing communication in light of this. What other kinds of analytical information do you need to research? Whom do you need to include from your team?

Be the Bard

In addition to using analytical information, it is crucial to energetically communicate with those you want to serve – customers, stakeholders, team members. Engaging your creativity is a great way to tap into the universal energies to get information you might not otherwise receive. It is no mistake that creativity is one of the energetic goals of the fifth chakra. Through your creative mind, you will find that the voice of your soul speaks to you.

Storytelling is a deeply creative process with an ancient history of telling inner truths in a symbolic way. Through your story, your energy goes out into the world and helps you co-create your reality. What business story do you want to write? What customers do you want to invite into your reality? Who do you want to take on your journey?

A bard is a medieval poet, storyteller, and musician. She represents that part of yourself that weaves together the threads of your soul story – your destiny. She reveals underlying truths and wisdom and helps you learn from your mistakes. Your inner bard helps you know when you are on the right path – or the wrong one. And she communicates your story to others on your path.

Once Upon a Business Dream

I invite you to become the bard and write your story about the business of your heart's desires – your dream business. You don't have to write a long story – one to three pages is just great. (In just a minute, we will quiet the inner mob that just erupted in chorus to object.)

Through creative storytelling, you may find your customer is a dragon, a fairy, or a robot. You yourself may take on an unexpected form such as a knight in shining armor or a sleek panther. Allow your creativity to flow from within. This is your story. You may choose to share it with others or not.

As an example, here is the start of my dream business story. "Once upon a time there was a business – but it looked more like a castle. The Queen of this amazing business was an incredible leader with a large heart and great wisdom, yet she didn't know how truly powerful she was. She had a compassionate and thoughtful soul and looked to attract many suitors (called customers) to her business. The business was located at the very heart of the village, and the Queen's supreme wish was to bring abundance in all forms, not only to her business, but also to the village at large."

Now it's time to quiet your inner mob so you can write your dream business story. Get several empty pieces of paper and a pen or pencil. Take one sheet and fill it with the clutter in your head from your inner mob. It doesn't have to make sense; just write and purge. When done, set it aside.

Now do the breathing meditation for the heart chakra. Afterward, take an empty sheet of paper and begin writing your story. There will be wisdom and understanding coming through your words. No need to force your story. Allow it to flow. If you feel stuck, try more breathing or perhaps a walk to clear your head. Keep writing until you feel like you are done. No matter how long or short your story is, it's perfect. You may decide to add on to it as things develop.

Once you are done, reread your story. What insights do you have? Is there any symbolism that resonates with you? If you are like me, you may find that greater understanding of your story unfolds as time goes on. Where do you see themes from your SWOT analysis that support your dream business? Where do you see you need to make changes? Pairing the creative voice of your soul with the perspective of your analytic mind, you will receive information for a more holistic approach to your business and your marketing message.

Putting It Into Practice

Susan, board chair for RIH, is sitting with Valerie in her office. Susan is prepared to have the hard conversation needed about what is happening at RIH. While Valerie is the CEO and founder of RIH, she is still under the authority of the Board of Directors.

Susan starts by stating clearly what she is observing at RIH. She cites the poor morale, decreasing profits, declining customer satisfaction, unsatisfactory goal attainment, and Valerie's obvious anger at her team. She asks Valerie what is at the heart of the issue. What is the underlying cause?

Valerie indicates that she has no idea why team members are behaving the way they are. She has tried everything she knows to make them do what they are supposed to.

Susan's antenna immediately goes up. She probes further and asks how Valerie is trying to get the team to do what they are supposed to. Valerie responds that her team is completely unqualified and difficult to manage. She would like to fire everyone and start over.

Since Susan was part of the interviewing process of team members, she knows for a fact that some of the most talented and qualified people around are currently working at RIH. She disagrees that everyone needs to be fired. A giant red flag goes up in Susan's mind.

She continues that she knows very little about Valerie's work history and would like to know more. Valerie shares a brief history in which she job-hopped a great deal. She explains this away by stating that leadership and co-workers were difficult, which is why she decided to do her own thing.

Susan looks directly at Valerie and asks the hard question. "How did you participate in the difficulties?" Valerie looks abashed. She claims no fault in the problems. "What did you do to try to solve the problems?" Susan continues. Valerie states that she felt there was no point in trying to resolve the problems, since everyone there was against her.

A pattern quickly emerges relating Valerie's history to the current situation at RIH. Susan points out that Valerie doesn't seem to want to work through the difficult situations at RIH, a tendency that is reflected in her employment history as well. Susan thinks Valerie would benefit from some communication and leadership classes. She feels sure the board would approve the funds for Valerie to take some.

Valerie abruptly stands up and leaves the office, slamming the door behind her. Susan looks out the window and sees Valerie driving away from RIH at top speed.

Susan, maintaining curiosity throughout the meeting, seeks to get information that will shed some light on the current situation at RIH. Through her sincere questions, she discovers some of the underlying issues. She values Valerie, and would like to see her succeed. However, she knows that Valerie is part of the problem and suggests a partial resolution through further educating Valerie.

Hard conversations don't always turn out the way one would like, and such is the case with Susan and Valerie. That said, the conversation isn't over, and both will have some time to regroup and pick up where they left off.

Taking Action

Now it's time for you to take action. Carry out the following activities to help you determine what your next steps need to be in order to be able to appropriately harness and exercise the fifth chakra power of your business.

1. Take the Chakra Assessment that follows and record your score. Does it indicate a glaring deficit in this chakra or just some tweaking?

2. Answer the Questions for Further Exploration that follows and write down any insights, new ideas, or awareness you may have.

3. Listen to the Play Your Music guided journey on the website and journal about your experience to: www.nanettegiacoma.com/OpenForBusinessBook.

4. Review the information and insights you have gathered from this chapter about the fifth chakra.

5. Read Ways to Balance Your Fifth Chakra, which follows, and select which things you want to try or make your own list of ideas.

6. From your list, choose 1-3 things you are going to do.

    a.___ What action steps will you take?

    b.___ Do you need help? What kind of help? From whom?

    c.___ When will you start? What is your goal completion date?

    d.___ How will you know you have reached your goal?

FIFTH CHAKRA ASSESSMENT

Fifth Chakra	Yes	No	Somewhat
Do you have open and honest communication with customers, business partners, and team members?			
Do you hold frequent, productive meetings with team members and other stakeholders?			
Do you encourage open dialogue with team members, customers, and other stakeholders? Even hard ones?			
Do you listen deeply to your own needs?			
Do you listen deeply to the needs of others?			
Do you clarify your understanding when someone is talking?			
Are you able to listen without interrupting?			

Do you give balanced positive and negative feedback to others?			
Do you refrain from gossiping or talking about others judgmentally?			
Do you have a strong and effective marketing message and strategy that bring in new customers?			
Do others understand when you talk about your business and what you do?			
Do you feel like you are fulfilling your business destiny?			
SCORE			

Give yourself 2 points for every Yes, 1 point for every Somewhat, and 0 points for No.

Scale: 4-12 points: Strong need for fifth chakra balancing

13-20 points: Some fifth chakra balancing needed

21-28 points: Congratulations! The fifth chakra of

your business is well-balanced.

Questions for Further Exploration

1. When do you communicate less than truthfully or authentically? Why?

2. How deeply do you listen to the needs of your customers and others? Describe what listening deeply means to you.

3. How frequently do you hold meetings? With whom? How productive and effective are they? What prevents you from having good meetings? How could they improve?

4. How effective are you at communicating your frustrations? What impacts this?

5. Are you ever verbally abusive? Who is this usually aimed at? How frequently do you criticize others? Yourself?

6. How could you better clarify what someone is talking about?

7. Are you ever wishy-washy? What happens when you agree with all sides of a debate or can't make a decision?

8. In what situations do you block your voice and remain silent? What are your fears about speaking out? Where do you feel them in your body?

9. Do you feel customers and others understand when you speak about your business and what you do? Describe where you think there is room for improvement.

10. Do you have a strong marketing strategy? How clear, creative, and effective are your marketing materials – website, business cards, social media, etc.? Describe.

11. How could you better tie in your core values with your business destiny?

Ways to Balance Your Fifth Chakra

✐ Business

❑ Ask for feedback from team members and others about your communication.

❑ Join a public speaking club.

❑ Take a communication class.

❑ Get communication training for your team.

❑ Do a team communication retreat.

❑ Make the time and effort to have the hard conversations to clear the air.

❑ Get a facilitator to help with hard team conversations.

❑ Learn the PeerSpirit Process and use it at your meetings.

❑ Write or update your dream business story.

❑ Get your team to write their stories about their dreams at work.

❑ Create or revamp your marketing message and materials.

❑ Create or revamp your marketing strategy and plan.

∽ **Body**

- ❑ Get a voice coach.
- ❑ Do neck and shoulder rolls.
- ❑ Get a neck and shoulder massage.
- ❑ With intention and consciousness, intone the vowels: a, e, i, o, u.
- ❑ Laugh (at jokes, funny movies, yourself, etc.).
- ❑ Sing or chant.
- ❑ Do mindful breathing in through the nose and out through the mouth.
- ❑ Practice mantra yoga.
- ❑ Eat fifth chakra foods.
- ❑ Diffuse or wear the following essential oils. For the throat: protective blend, melaleuca, or oregano. For the thyroid: myrrh, or peppermint. For the ears: helichrysum, basil, or melaleuca.

∽ **Emotions**

- ❑ Express something you normally wouldn't.
- ❑ Practice saying things in advance that are difficult or important.
- ❑ Practice speaking your truth.
- ❑ Journal about your feelings.
- ❑ Write or tell stories.
- ❑ Scream to release feelings (in your car, a secluded place, but not at anyone).
- ❑ Take an art class.
- ❑ Do inner child work and allow your inner child to "speak."
- ❑ Participate in group therapy or other personal growth groups.
- ❑ Diffuse or wear the following essential oils: black pepper, spearmint, cassia jasmine, or lavender.

∽ **Energy**

- ❑ Wear turquoise or other blue stones.
- ❑ Wear blue clothing.
- ❑ Spend time clarifying your destiny at this time in your life.
- ❑ Practice mindful listening meditations.

❑ Carry out silent observation.

❑ Practice an art on a daily or weekly basis.

❑ Listen to music in the key of G.

❑ Sing or chant.

❑ Use rhythmic instruments.

❑ Learn or play a musical instrument.

❑ Diffuse or wear the following essential oils: ylang-ylang, lavender, Roman chamomile, gardenia, or frankincense.

ᑲ Affirmations for the Fifth Chakra

❑ I am creative.

❑ I comfortable expressing myself.

❑ I am honest and open.

❑ I speak my truth.

❑ I express myself clearly.

❑ I hear purely.

❑ I hear deeply.

❑ I am fulfilling my destiny.

❑ I communicate with true authenticity.

Guided Journey: Play Your Music

Imagine you are standing high on a mountain late in the afternoon. A light, warm mist sprinkles you with a thousand wet, loving kisses. It feels delicious and sensual. Look around and fully take in the mountain you're standing on. What does it look like? Taste the air. Listen to the mountain. What does it communicate to you? What other sounds do you hear? What is the quality of the mountain's vibration? How does it resonate with the vibration of your own authentic voice? Or not?

Look down the side of the mountain. Far below lies a vast valley of bright, sky-blue irises. Indeed, it seems the sky lies below you instead of above. The sun peeks through the thin, low clouds, illuminating the mist into tiny, tiny crystals that sparkle across the sky. As it does, color floods the sky, and an enormous rainbow spans the valley. Pause and wonder at this magnificent view.

You are filled with the desire to further explore the magic and mystery of the valley. To your right there is a circuitous stone path that leads down the mountain. Intuitively, you know that it leads to a place beneath the rainbow. As you step upon the stones, you notice there are symbols engraved into them resembling the oracle rune stones of the ancient Vikings. There is enormous energy emanating from each stone.

You feel the vibration of the mountain come up through the soles of your feet and continue moving through your body. Feel its warmth enter the bottom of your feet and move slowly up your body. When it reaches your throat, allow the vibration to pause there. Feel it in your jaw, ears, and across your shoulders.

You walk the path of the rune stones for some time. Each step takes you closer to finding the vibration of your true voice, authentic creativity, and pure communication in all forms. Listening deeply, you begin to find clarity in the whisperings of the stones.

Finally, you arrive at the bottom of the mountain, where you find yourself knee-deep in sky-blue irises, the path barely visible through the swaying flowers. The rainbow above you seems so close that you try to touch it, but it is out of reach. You slowly meander through the irises. Their heady fragrance releases any lingering tension in your jaw, neck, and shoulders.

You immerse yourself in your walking meditation in this sacred sanctuary. Here you are able to fully own what you need to heal and balance your throat chakra. Where do you feel the imbalances? Is there excessive or deficient energy? Listen deeply. What does your inner divine voice tell you?

With your next step, the stone pathway stops abruptly. You look up and discover that you are standing directly beneath the rainbow. Either end of it stretches out as far as the eye can see. The energy of the rainbow pulls at you from above – gently at first and then with more intensity, until you are lifted off the ground. Do you resist or do you allow yourself to float freely? A tingle of energy spreads through your body as you pass through the colors of the rainbow. You finally come to rest on the bright-blue stripe.

Turn around and take in the view from this height. Take a moment to breathe and meditate on the sounds. What messages await you? You take one more deep breath, and as you exhale, you hear the sweet sound of chimes. In the next instant, the goddess Iris appears before you. She is the messenger of the gods, linking the spirit realm and humanity. She radiates truth and purity. Notice all you can about this divine being.

With her, she carries a clear blue pouch that looks as if it holds the sky. She speaks to you in a gently musical voice. She says, "Within this bag lies your musical instrument, one given to you by the Great Divine the day you were born. It vibrates with the music of your authentic voice."

She invites you to reach inside the bag. When you do, you find there are many instruments to choose from, but only one of them is yours. Which do you choose? You innately know how to play this instrument. You require no lessons.

"Go ahead," Iris says, "Play your instrument! It is your divine right! Play it now."

When you play your instrument, you hear the music of your soul, releasing your divine truth, self-expression, and destiny. Listen to the sound of your beautiful music. Feel its vibration in your fifth chakra. What message does it bring to you? What message do you need to share with the world?

The goddess smiles and tells you it is time for you to bring your music into the world. She gives you a playful little push and sends you sliding down the rainbow. You have the ability to determine how quickly or slowly you descend. Before long, you find you've landed in the field of irises. In the distance, you notice the mountain where you started your journey. How does it look from where you now stand? Do you hear it speaking to you?

As you listen, it begins to shimmer and fade. From somewhere, you hear the chimes of the goddess. When you hear the final ringing of the chimes, you will come back to ordinary reality.

❧ Notes ❧

❧ Notes ❧

❦ CHAPTER 8 ❦
Sixth Chakra: Dreamweaver

Every great dream begins with a dreamer.
Always remember, you have within you the strength,
the patience, and the passion to reach for
the stars to change the world.

Harriet Tubman

CHAKRA 6 QUICK REFERENCE GUIDE

SIXTH CHAKRA	CORRELATIONS
Sanskrit Name	Ajna
Meaning	Perceive, command, beyond wisdom
Location	Between the eyes at the brow
In the Body Governs	The head, brain, nervous system, and all sense organs
Endocrine Gland	Pituitary
Imbalances	Headaches, vision problems, seizures, insomnia, nausea, sinus issues, anxiety, being overwhelmed, or mental exhaustion; also, over-intellectualization, over-thinking, seeing yourself in a bad light, being controlling or perfectionistic; poor memory, or difficulty concentrating; shortsighted about life or living in a fantasy world; no dream recall or lack of imagination
Energetic Goals	Balance between left (rational, thinking) and right (intuitive, creative) brain for a whole brain approach; open-mindedness, insight, clear vision, strong intuition, strong dream recall, symbolic thinking, and a healthy imagination; seeing yourself as a fluid, spiritual being, able to co-create with your Higher Power
Rights	I see, I imagine, I understand
Color	Indigo blue
Food	None. Try fasting for a day to clean out your body

Element	Light
Stones	Lapis Lazuli
Animal	Owl
Archetype	Seer, psychic, or dreamer
Plant	Almond blossom
Music	Musical note A
Essential Oil	Clary sage, coriander, lemongrass

Are you a Dreamweaver? Do you seek meaning in your sleeping dreams? Do you daydream? Are you open to receiving symbolic messages from your guides, angels, your Higher Power, the Universe? Are you co-dreaming your business into reality? If so, then you are definitely a Dreamweaver. If not, no worries. You too can easily become a Dreamweaver.

Dreams have a rich history dating back thousands of years as a means of gaining knowledge and wisdom and as prophecies. Symbols and archetypes are the language of dreams. Through these symbols and archetypes, your dreams speak to your unconscious mind, and your conscious mind helps you interpret their meaning.

C.G. Jung, the well-known psychologist, extensively researched dreams – his own and those of his patients. He used them as a means of gaining understanding about his own personal psyche and insight into his patients' issues. He worked extensively with the collective unconscious when working with dreams and in his waking life as well.

The collective unconscious consists of universal symbols and archetypes. Examples of universal archetypes are the wise woman, divine child, great mother, trickster, hero, etc. These archetypes exist in most ancient cultures exclusive of interaction with each other. So, before the internet and the World Wide Web, humans shared an energetic psychic web that transcended cultures. This is the third eye (sixth) chakra at work.

When you tap into the psychic web, you will discover that your guides, angels, god/dess, Higher Power, etc., are trying to speak to you through the language of signs and symbols. It is my experience that when I see, hear, or notice a sign or symbol three times, I need to pay attention. Or sometimes the sign is so BIG, I can't miss it!

Several years ago, while on my daily walk in our field, a grouse flew out of the woods and landed in my path. It flapped its wings wildly while squawking loudly. It did its crazy dance all around me. I changed my route immediately and gave it a wide berth. There was no doubt in my mind that it was protecting its nest egg. I also knew it was a sign! The grouse was alerting me that someone was threatening my nest egg.

At the time, my husband and I were partnering with a man to create a nonprofit. We were footing the bill until things got up and running. Our partner would give me receipts for related expenses to be reimbursed. As I reviewed the recent receipts our partner had given me, I realized there was a significant increase in expenses. However, I couldn't find all the items purchased. There were also some very expensive items included, like a computer, that hadn't been discussed. It was time for a hard conversation!

I questioned our partner in more detail about the money being spent. Had the grouse not crossed my path, I might have believed him when he said the computer and other items were accidentally included for reimbursement. But my intuition was heightened, and I "knew" he was lying. Reviewing some past receipts, it became apparent that our partner had been subtly stealing from us over the past few months. We instantly parted ways.

You never know how a sign or symbol will appear. My sister-in-law has received some great messages reading vanity plates on cars while sitting in traffic, while mine often come in the form of animals. I always pay attention to what animals are present when I am outdoors, especially if one keeps showing up over the course of weeks or months.

I knew I was in trouble when a family of foxes moved in nearby and ate our chickens. In the same timeframe, I had to swerve to avoid foxes that repeatedly ran in front of my car. The fox is often a trickster symbol, and it certainly was for me. I ended up making a series of expensive mistakes over the next year that included an auto accident (it totaled my car and the other driver's, but fortunately no one was seriously hurt) and spilling liquid on not one, but two computers (one of which was not mine)!

Apparently my Higher Power decided I needed a lesson about forgiving myself (I'm a bit of a perfectionist) and receiving forgiveness. In all instances, I was grateful that I had the resources to cover the expenses, and all the people involved in my mistakes were amazingly kind, generous, and forgiving (even the other driver and the police). Fortunately, the foxes have moved further into the woods, and my mistakes have gotten less expensive.

If you are asking for guidance or praying for help, and you don't feel like you are getting it, try allowing your unconscious mind be your guide. How many times have you written off a sign or symbol as a coincidence or an anomaly? Paying attention is the most important part of receiving signs and symbols. Be on the lookout!

As part of a daily practice, start noticing signs and symbols that come your way. What keeps showing up? What catches your attention? Do you keep seeing the same car, word, person, image, or animal? How do they relate to you? What do you need to know at this time? What are you seeking to learn? If you open yourself up to universal communication, you will begin wakeful dreaming. By that I mean tapping into the universal language of signs and symbols.

Don't let your rational brain talk you out of the wisdom you are receiving. It may not initially make sense to your conscious mind. Just like learning a new foreign language, it may take some time for you to catch on to what is being conveyed. If you need some help, a book on symbols might help, or Google a sign or symbol and see if anything resonates with you.

In the Notes section of this chapter, write about signs or symbols you have noticed. Did you pay attention to them? Did you act on them? What happened as a result?

Imagine You're a Dreamer

Have you ever woken up from a dream thinking, "Well, that was just plain weird!" Typically dreams are not literal. Their meaning lies in the symbols and archetypes and how they relate to you and your situation. The dreaming mind doesn't have the same sense of reality that your waking mind has.

Indeed, there are mystic traditions that don't distinguish reality in terms of sleeping or waking. They are both are considered a dream reality. Some Native American traditions consider the sleeping dream to be more real in terms of important sacred messages that will help guide your life.

The Dreamer is one of the sixth chakra archetypes, and for good reason. Through your dreams, you can reveal your personal mythology. Dreams have a way of consolidating your life experiences, conflicts, cultural biases, childhood wounding, spirituality, etc. They offer an opportunity to get a different perspective on yourself and your situation.

While your conscious mind feels like it is in control of your thoughts and actions, it only controls about five to ten percent of your mind. Most of your thoughts and actions are controlled by your subconscious mind, which is the pre-programmed mind. It is the part of your mind that learns through experience. It determines what is "true" through your repetitive experiences.

It is also the mind that will steer you to repeat actions and behaviors because they feel familiar and safe to the subconscious mind. The subconscious mind doesn't distinguish between actions that are productive and those that are counterproductive for you at this point in your life. These actions are often linked to the voices of the inner mob. Often you aren't even aware of your behaviors in relation to the inner mob, hence the term subconscious – "below consciousness".

The third level of consciousness is the unconscious mind. This is your dreaming mind. It speaks to you in signs and symbols in your sleeping dreams and imagination. Through it, you are able to step outside of your habitual thinking and see yourself, your life, and your business with less distortion and more accuracy. That's why it's important to pay attention to your dreams.

There are three categories of dreams that may be helpful in evaluating the type of dream you're having. First, self-limiting dreams reinforce your belief or myth that you are somehow flawed. What are some of your self-limiting beliefs? Are you a failure, poor, disempowered, etc.? Have you ever dreamed you were being pursued by bad people? Or that you had forgotten to get dressed and were now at work in your underwear? I have!

New myth dreams help you create a new and improved story about yourself. For example, you might counter a self-limiting failure myth by dreaming you are incredibly successful at your business.

An integration dream may help you integrate your old self-limiting myth with a new myth. Perhaps you dream of a solution to a conflict you are currently having, or you have an "aha" moment that assists you on your path to success.

Your self-limiting myths frequently result in counterproductive behaviors and actions in your personal life and your business. So, if you examine your dreams and work through the messages contained within them, it will benefit you in all areas of your life and business.

Dreamcatcher

How do you capture the wisdom of your sleeping dreams? Perhaps you already have a rich dream life that you tap into readily. If not, here are a few tips to help. First and foremost, set your intention to remember your dreams. You may simply set your intention in your mind, or you might want to formally write it down. To strengthen your intention, go to the Notes section of this chapter and write down your intention to remember your dreams and your desire to seek wisdom from the messages therein.

Before you go to sleep each night, do a breathing meditation for a few minutes, as described in Chapter 4. Notice where you are tense and breathe into those places, releasing your tension on the exhalation. Repeat ten to twenty times, "I will remember a dream upon waking." You may want to ask for insight or understanding about a problem or issue in your life or business before going to sleep.

Place a journal beside your bed so you can readily capture your dream upon waking. Allow yourself to wake slowly. If you wake with an alarm, try using a gentle tone that will be less jarring. Take a few moments and hold the dream in your mind. Then write down the dream in the present tense, as if it is happening right now.

Write down whatever comes to you, even if it is only an impression you have of the dream, a fragment, or a feeling. By writing down whatever comes to you, you may remember more of the dream or your unconscious mind may help you imagine what you need to know even if you don't remember the whole dream. Consider allowing your unconscious mind to finish your dream for you if it is unclear.

Record as many details of the dream as possible, and what they mean to you personally. Are there colors, symbols, people, animals that have meaning for you? Pay particular attention to how you feel. Feelings are a great indicator of the function of the dream. Are you scared, happy, confused, peaceful, etc.? Do your feelings relate to a current self-limiting belief? A new possibility? Or integrating an old myth with a new one?

Remember, dreams are usually about you. So, if you dream about a person you know, ask yourself what that person has to do with where and who you are right now. For example, I will invariably dream about my husband when I need to tap into my masculine energy. I have dreamed on multiple occasions that my mother died, even though she is alive and well. The symbolic message is that I need to release some aspect of the subconscious programming I learned from my mother as a child.

Continue your dreaming by writing about possible messages and insights you have about your dream. Let the images, colors, and feelings speak to you through free association. For example, if I dream I'm driving in a car, I might write down the car make, model, year, condition, or color. Other free associations are: on the road again, travel, how I get around, metal, in the driver's seat, going nowhere, etc. Play with free-associating the dream and see where it takes you.

You might also start an imaginary conversation between the things and/ or characters in your dream. For example, if I dream that I'm in my car with my mother, I might ask my mother what she's doing in my dream and why we are driving around in my car. Or I might ask my car what message it has for me. As I write down the answers, I gain insight into the symbolic messages in the dream.

Through your unconscious mind, your dreams provide fresh insights because they bypass your inner mob, who are stuck in the beliefs of your subconscious mind. By following your dreams, you will begin to see patterns that will inform you, whether those patterns indicate self-limiting myths, new myths, or myths in transition.

Have some fun with this. Dreams are fascinating and will take you places you never dreamed of.

Dream Catcher Mandala

Use a template to draw a circle on a blank piece of paper or cardboard. A paper plate, pie tin, or pizza stone will do nicely, depending on how big you want your circle. Cut out the paper circle with scissors or a utility knife if using cardboard. Fill the circle with an indigo blue color using a pen, pencil, paint, or marker. This represents your sixth chakra. Draw, paint, or glue images and symbols within the circle that capture a dream (remembered or imagined). This is not a replication of your dream, just an impression. Focus on how the dream made you feel and allow that to inform your process.

You may wish to use pictures from magazines or found objects from nature or other sources such as leaves, feathers, seeds, buttons, ribbon, glitter, etc. Use one or more colors. The cardboard works best if you plan on gluing heavier objects on your mandala. Let go of the VOJ (Voice of Judgment) and allow yourself free rein. This is not supposed to be a great work of art, just an opportunity for you to use your dreaming mind.

Once you are done, write about your mandala in the Notes section of this chapter. Allow yourself the freedom to write whatever comes to you. Write faster than you can think. Let your hand write the words instead of your conscious mind. Pay no attention to grammar, punctuation, or spelling, and don't worry about whether it makes sense or not. Continue writing about your mandala until you feel you have received the intended message. Then review what you have written.

What insights, wisdom, and intuitions do you have about your dream catcher mandala? How does this apply to your life and business at this time? How will you integrate this information? Keep this information handy for use in the Taking Action section of this chapter.

The Oracle of Your Business

How often have you wished you had a crystal ball or that you were an oracle and knew the future of your business or a solution to a problem or the best answer to an important decision?

The truth is you are indeed your own oracle. The sixth chakra is called the third eye chakra because it is the energetic center of your psychic abilities. The psychic is a sixth chakra archetype. If you feel your third eye is closed, it is likely you haven't been trained to use your psychic abilities, or you may have been taught to ignore them in favor of using only your rational or analytic mind. Such is the case for many people in our culture.

Intuition or psychic abilities draw on the oneness of the Universe to focus on the whole rather than the parts. You look for the interconnection and similarities between seemingly unrelated things and trust that there is meaning in the correlation, even if it doesn't make sense to your rational brain.

Just because you don't know how to use your third eye, that doesn't mean you can't. You may even be using it without realizing it. As with a new technology, you sometimes have to experiment or be taught how to use your psychic abilities. Think back to when the internet first came into being. It's likely you took some time to learn how to use it. Like the internet, you have to explore how to use your psychic abilities.

In business, psychic ability is often couched in terms like "gut instincts" or "business intuition." Do you rely on your gut instincts or your business intuition? If so, you are tapping into the energy of your third eye.

There are different types of psychic knowing. They are called the "clairs." The clairs are about how you receive intuitive information. There is clairvoyance, clairaudience, clairsentience, and claircognizance. You may already be using one or more of these. As I discuss the clairs in more detail, notice if one or more of the descriptions sounds familiar to you.

In My Mind's Eye

Clairvoyance is what is commonly mistaken as the only psychic ability. This is the ability to visually see an image or scene in your mind's eye or imagination. These images may come to you unbidden and leave you wondering about their meaning. Like dreams, these images are often symbolic, not literal. If you dream vividly in colorful detail, you may have a propensity towards this clair.

For example, you may be thinking of developing a business partnership with someone, and an image of a dog jumps into your mind. It will depend on your association with dogs, but for me it would mean this person is loyal like a dog and belongs in my pack.

Oracle and tarot cards are a great way to practice your clairvoyance. The images will tap into your inner seeing and allow messages to reach you in ways your rational brain doesn't grasp. They are useful for exploring the outcome of potential decisions, gaining more information about a situation or a person, and, most importantly, pursuing self-discovery.

There are several spreads you can use with one, three, six, or more cards. Most oracle and tarot decks will give you examples of these in the accompanying booklets. I have about twenty different decks, and I use all of them. Sometimes I'll use two decks at once to get different perspectives on the same situation.

To do a card reading, start by calling in your guides, angels, or Higher Power or do a short breathing meditation to clear your mind. Then ask an open-ended question. For example, "What will be the outcome of partnering with Connie Clarence for XYZ project?" Shuffle the cards while holding the question in your mind. Pull one or more cards.

What do you notice first about the cards you pull? What draws your attention? What feelings, memories, or thoughts do they spark? I recommend allowing yourself to interpret the images on the cards rather than reading what is written about them in the booklets. In this way, you are developing and relying on your inner seeing for answers.

You can also use this to help you gain insight into how to approach a hard conversation with a person, how to approach a new client, or just for any situation about which you would like more information. I also have a few oracle deck apps on my phone for on-the-go questions. I find that pulling a card or two really helps me navigate issues when my rational brain is feeling overwhelmed.

I Hear You

Clairaudience is inner hearing and is often received as a voice of wisdom in your mind. You can distinguish this voice from the inner mob because it will be clear, calm, and nonjudgmental. Your inner oracle will not tell you what you "ought" to do or how you "should" proceed. She will not create drama, make you feel small, or try to guilt or shame you. Often the messages are simple and straightforward.

For example, I awoke one morning to a clear voice that said, "Wisdom's daughter leads the way." I knew it was a message encouraging me to follow my inner wisdom and help other women learn to hear and trust their inner wisdom – one of my favorite ways to work with my clients!

Notice if you can distinguish between the voices of your inner mob and the quiet voice of your inner guidance. If your mob is loud, stop the inner dialogue, take a deep breath, and clear your mind. Every time you catch yourself listening to the inner mob, take a moment to let your mind go blank.

Each time, listen for the silence in the blank spaces between the inner noise. What do you hear? Some people may initially hear a subtle buzzing, but allow your awareness to find the silence behind that. Come back to the silent space over and over, and strengthen your ability to listen for the quiet voice of your intuition. Try to catch the whispering voice of your intuition. Make a note of it so you will recognize your intuitive voice in the future.

It will definitely help if you have a regular meditation practice. This will aid in quieting your inner mob and strengthening your ability to hear your intuition. Messages may come while meditating or they may come later, but if you continue to practice deep listening, you will ultimately receive the answers you need.

Can't Stop the Feeling

Clairsentience is when you receive a message through a feeling. This is your gut instinct or business intuition – you may get a feeling that you need to proceed in a certain way, contact a person, or avoid someone or something.

I remember years ago, when I was a skilled nursing facility administrator, I needed to hire a bookkeeper. I had several viable applicants with great qualifications. I called each for an interview. During one of the phone calls, I had the distinct feeling I would hire that applicant. I still conducted all the interviews, but, at the end of the day, I hired the woman about whom I had the intuitive feeling. She turned out to be outstanding! After I moved on, she continued to grow personally and professionally, and she eventually became an administrator. To this day, I keep in touch with her through Facebook.

You also tap into your clairsentience when you feel the mood of a room you just walked into. Some people who are particularly sensitive to clairsentient energy will pick up the emotional or physical feelings of others. They may become happy, sad, discouraged, etc., depending on who they are engaging with. For example, their stomach might feel queasy if they are near a nervous person.

When working with Reiki clients, I will often feel their discomfort and energetic imbalances. When those feelings are particularly strong, I quickly ground my energy and direct them earthward so as not to become overwhelmed or dizzy with the energy they contain.

If you have ever felt drained emotionally or energetically while in the company of a friend, colleague, or family member, it is probable you are tapping into their inner physical or emotional feelings.

Bubble Up!

If you are prone to taking on the energy of others, an energy bubble is an easy and effective way to protect yourself. Start by facing your slightly cupped hands towards each other. Place them at heart level. Imagine holding a small invisible bubble of energy between them. Move your hands in and out a bit until you feel the energy pulsing. If you can't feel it, no worries; it's still there.

Enlarge the invisible energy bubble so that it can easily encompass your entire body. Step into it so you are surrounded with energy. With your hands, scoop earth energy up from the ground and sweep it up the front of your body until your hands are over your head. Arc your hands and arms back down to the floor with the downward arm movement of a jumping jack.

You are now enveloped in an invisible bubble of energy, and only positive energy can enter. All negative or unwanted energy will bounce off. Consider using the energy bubble when you know you will be with challenging people or when you will be in large crowds.

I Know What I Know

Claircognizance is an inner knowing. It feels a bit like information being downloaded into your head. Think about a computer program update, and you get the idea. You will just suddenly "know" something. When my husband loses his keys, I like using this method best of all. I ask, "If I were Pete's keys, where would I be?" I immediately know they are in the hamper. I tell him, "Your keys are in the hamper." He responds, "I checked the hamper." I look in the hamper, and there they are – in the pocket of his jeans in the hamper.

Try this method when faced with a business question to which your rational brain can't find an answer. Perhaps you've been trying to figure out the best way to achieve a challenging goal. Ask your intuition, "How can I achieve this goal?" What information download do you get?

Ways of working with your intuition that might be useful if you think you tend to be claircognizant are numerology, astrology, sacred geometry, and quantum physics. Each of these tends to blend science and mysticism. They will feed the desire of the left brain to know and understand in rational ways and help make the connection with the mysterious energy of the unknown in the right brain.

Practice Makes Psychic

As with most things in life and business, the more you practice something, the more natural it becomes. Intuition and/or psychic abilities are no different. They are innate. Everyone has these abilities. They can be learned, and there are many books and classes available to help you further develop your intuition. Some are listed in the resource section of this book.

You can start by noticing how you usually receive intuitive information. How does it come in? Do you see it in your mind's eye? Can you hear your guides whispering to you? Perhaps you just get a feeling about it or you just know.

Flex your psychic muscle every time you are about to enter a business meeting by pausing outside the door. Notice any intuitions you have about the room, people, and situation. When you step through the doorway, notice any new impressions you have. How does this affect you energetically? Do you enter a new state of awareness? How does this information come to you?

Another great way to bone up psychically is to pick up a deck of oracle or tarot cards that speak to you visually and pull one daily. Write about your insights or impressions and how the card applies to your life or business. Daily use of a pendulum is a great way to help you make yes/no decisions intuitively. See whether you think your pendulum ultimately directs you towards the best option.

Other possibilities are to use numerology to help you learn about yourself, your life, your business. Get your astrological chart done, and pay attention to the changes in your life and business accordingly. See a psychic and notice what rings true and false for you.

In the Notes section of this chapter, write down a simple business question to which you would like the answer. Close your eyes, and take a few meditative breaths. Do you notice any changes in your awareness? What does your business intuition tell you? What download do you receive? How does your inner wise woman speak to you? What images come to mind? Notice the way the answer comes to you. How will you act on this information? Write about your experience.

The Tao of Decision-Making

A balance between left brain rational-analytic thinking and right brain intuitive-creative thinking is one of the energetic goals of the sixth chakra, and it is ideal for a whole brain approach to decision-making. This is based in the Taoist philosophy of yin-yang energy that was discussed in Chapter 5 in reference to the third chakra.

Using a fluid yin-yang decision-making model will help you change with the needs of your team, the business, and the larger community. You will respond more successfully to unexpected and uncontrollable events. By balancing your left brain–right brain abilities, you will better understand the essential nature of an issue and therefore make the best decision possible.

Albert Einstein observed, "The significant problems we face cannot be solved at the same level of thinking we were at when we created them." Where would Albert Einstein be if he had not delved into his yin side and dreamt of how molecules work so he could later put that notion into practice through experiments?

Similarly, you will make better decisions if you allow your creative-intuitive dreaming mind to go outside the set parameters of rational-analytic thinking. Ideally, you will allow an open-minded dance between the opposing yin-yang energies. Allowing your mind to participate fully often requires that normal boundaries be dissolved so you can delve into your creativity. Then new solutions can be implemented with the help of the rational mind.

Daniel Pink, in his book *A Whole New Mind*, goes to great lengths to help us understand why using both our right and left brain is so important in what he calls the dawning of the conceptual age. He states, "The most creative among us see relationships the rest of us never notice. Such ability is at a premium in a world where specialized knowledge work can quickly become routinized work – and therefore be automated or outsourced away."

Yin and yang are interdependent upon each other for balance. It is the oscillation between the two energies that is so conducive to great decision-making. It is the push of yang and the pull of yin that cause your thinking to become dynamic and flexible so that you can access your full potential for brilliant decisions.

The *Tao Te Ching* states, "Do your work, then step back." In terms of decision-making, this is a great philosophy. You need reflection time to analyze how your actions are affecting your business, and you need creative time so you can respond to the constant fluctuations around you.

It is important to do systematic analysis and get a reliable set of data to help make decisions. Data helps you make SMART goals and define new markets. It is great for seeing where you have been in relation to where you want to go. Data is useful in helping prevent undesirable outcomes and predicting future trends. Currently there is more data available through the World Wide Web than you can possibly digest. You may even drive yourself a little crazy trying to sift through it all. But it is a great way to get your rational-analytic left brain involved in the decision process.

That said, you need to step back from the analysis and allow the right brain to holistically gather all the pieces together, both the analytic data and the intuitive impressions that come to you. Do you have any gut responses to the information you gathered? Do you have a vision that seems outside of the realm of possibility based on what you have discovered? How can you find the clarity you desire?

Perhaps pulling a few oracle or tarot cards will help you discover a new way of seeing the data. Maybe you want to look at the numbers in terms of the data and numerology. Does that pie chart have any relation to something in sacred geometry? Try using a pendulum to help make a yes/no decision easier. Ask your dreams, guides, or Higher Power for some help seeing the big picture and to give you the insight you need to make the best decision possible. And then pay attention to the answers you receive.

Trust the Process

When I was working on my second Masters in Art and Consciousness Studies, my professors would say, "Trust the process," meaning don't worry about the outcome. What is most important is being present to what you are experiencing. What do you need to learn in this moment? Allow your awareness to transcend the boundaries of your conscious and subconscious minds to participate in the great universal wisdom available through the dreamweaving of the unconscious mind.

Through the exercises in this book, you are in "the process." Perhaps you picked up this book with the hope of growing personally, and professionally, or maybe you hope to grow your business. All good goals. But the most important thing you can do for yourself is trust that the process will take you where you need to go. You may end up getting exactly what you wanted from this book, but more likely you will end up someplace even better. Someplace you didn't even know you needed to go but that will enrich you and your business in ways you didn't even imagine.

By doing the assessments, exercises, and guided journeys and by creating the mandalas in this book, you are trusting your sixth chakra process to tap into your inner Dreamweaver. Whatever you receive through these processes will be exactly what you need. Maybe it will be a feeling, a thought, a vision, or just a vague understanding that you need to be doing something different. Or maybe you will have an even stronger conviction to continue on your current path. Regardless, know that your sixth chakra is bringing you the fruits of your psychic intuition through your process.

The guided journeys and the mandalas in particular are conducive to helping you tap into your sixth chakra insights. Guided journeys are a form of lucid dreaming. Lucid dreaming is a state in which the dreamer is conscious she is dreaming and has some control over how the dream proceeds. It is an opportunity to use your active imagination and, at the same time, receive symbolic messages along the way.

Mandalas are considered by some to be the sacred geometry of meditation. They are a great way to allow your mind to relax and be in the present moment. In the process, you silence the chatter of the inner mob. True insight and deep awareness can come from this quieting, meditative practice.

Sometimes the hardest thing to do is to relax and trust that the process is going to take you where you need to go. Trust that the information, the impressions, and the insights will serve you in your life and business. It is not always immediately apparent how your insights will be applied, yet they will. Sometimes it is with twenty-twenty hindsight that I realize how a dream or a message impacted my life. This is why it is important to keep a journal and record your impressions, insights, creative imaginings, and intuitions.

For example, I had a dream several years ago in which I am walking into a bazaar of vendors selling a variety of things. A small, ancient woman with wispy white hair calls me over. She wears a shapeless brown dress and a big toothless smile as she stands behind her nearly empty vendor's table. She asks me, "Why aren't you doing your work?" "I haven't been called," I reply.

She leans her head back and yells in an amplified voice, "Naaannnnettte!" The sound reverberates around the whole bazaar. I stand there silently, feeling stunned and humbled. She then tells me to choose something off her table. I choose a thinly sliced piece of coconut and eat it. It feels like a sacred act, and I realize I'm committing to my higher calling.

She then instructs me to go around the corner to another vendor. Not knowing exactly where I am going, I set off. When I see a table filled with handmade masks, I know I've found what I need to see.

Upon waking, the dream seemed surreal. I knew I was being asked to remove my masks and show up more authentically. The ancient woman appeared to be a shaman of sorts who was initiating me into the next phase of my life, but I didn't know what that meant.

At the time, I was doing some consulting work with a company where there was the possibility of becoming a permanent, full-time employee. Ultimately, it didn't work out. I stepped down from the process, realizing that it wasn't my path, even though I didn't know exactly what my next steps were.

Only now, years later, do I see the benefits of the spiraling path that brought me to where I am today – and my path continues to spiral in new directions. I move ever closer to my calling – walking between the worlds of executive coaching and alternative healing. And that dream stays with me every step of the way. It is a reminder that I have been called to my work, even when there are big challenges.

Shift through your notes about the guided journeys you have done so far in this book. Reflect on the process. In the Notes section of this chapter, write down questions, themes, or any other insights you may have from your collective journeys.

Now spend some time sitting and looking at your mandalas. Review your notes about your mandalas. What new questions, themes, or insights do you have from your creative process?

Putting It Into Practice

Megan is dreaming that a huge red dragon is flying over the town. It breathes bright orange and yellow flames that scorch the houses and trees. People are running for their lives. There seems to be nowhere to hide. Megan is terrified.

From behind a cloud of smoke, an even bigger green dragon appears. Initially, Megan feels a sense of doom, but then she notices the green dragon shooting blue and green flames at the red dragon. When the flames of the green dragon interact with the flames of the red dragon, they turn to rain that quenches the many fires set by the breath of the red dragon.

People of the town start cheering, and eventually the green dragon chases the red dragon back into the cave from which it came. Megan realizes everything will be okay, and she wakes up with an enormous sense of relief.

Megan has been journaling about her dreams over the last few months. Many have been filled with images of pursuit and feelings of fear. This is the first dream that gives her a sense of hope.

She knows it reflects her recent actions at the board meeting, when she spoke from her heart about the issues at Rainbow Integrated Health. She is feeling empowered (the green dragon) and prepared to take on the wrath of the red dragon (Valerie). She is unwilling to continue working under the current conditions.

With the help of the message in her dream, Megan is clear about what she must do if the RIH team is to be saved. She also knows there is going to be a confrontation with Valerie that will result in a very, very hard conversation. Whereas Megan has previously backed down in the face of Valerie's wrath, she will now stand her ground. Tomorrow is Monday, and Megan is ready to face the challenges and the consequences that the day will bring.

Over the last few months, Megan has been having dreams that reinforced a self-limiting myth, but her most recent dream is a new myth dream. In it she releases her self-limiting belief of powerlessness and rises as a powerful dragon that is able to defend not only herself, but her teammates as well.

Megan knows to trust the dream process. She is prepared to embody her new inner myth. She is ready and willing to change her actions and behaviors to create a new outer myth that will match her new inner myth. She must become the symbolic green dragon. There will be challenges and obstacles, but she will meet each from her heart center while expressing herself authentically and honestly.

Up to now, the success of the organization has been impeded by the lower chakra energy of RIH team members and Valerie's ability to create fear and overpower and control others. The energy at RIH will shift based on Megan's actions. Not only is Megan's dream a new myth dream for herself, but at some intuitive level she knows it will save the team as well.

Taking Action

Now it's time for you to take action. Carry out the following activities to help you determine what your next steps need to be in order to be able to appropriately harness and exercise the sixth chakra power of your business.

1. Take the Chakra Assessment that follows and record your score. Does it indicate a glaring deficit in this chakra or just some tweaking?

2. Answer the Questions for Further Exploration that follows and write down any insights, new ideas, or awareness you may have.

3. Listen to the Moon Pool guided journey on the website and journal about your experience: www.nanettegiacoma.com/OpenForBusinessBook.

4. Review the information and insights you have gathered from this chapter about the sixth chakra.

5. Read Ways to Balance Your Sixth Chakra, which follows, and select which things you want to try or make your own list of ideas.

6. From your list, choose 1-3 things you are going to do.

   a.___ What action steps will you take?

   b.___ Do you need help? What kind of help? From whom?

   c.___ When will you start? What is your goal completion date?

   d.___ How will you know you have reached your goal?

SIXTH CHAKRA ASSESSMENT

Sixth Chakra	Yes	No	Somewhat
Do you believe you have good business instincts or intuition?			
Do you take action based on your instincts and intuition?			
Do you balance intuitive and rational thinking when making decisions?			
Are you able to get emotionally neutral and mentally quiet to tap into your intuition?			
Do you seek wisdom from the signs and symbols that appear?			
Are you clear about your business intentions?			
Do you engage in visualizations, daydreams, making vision boards, or other imaginings about your business?			
Do you think others understand your vision for your business?			
Do you remember your dreams? Are they vivid?			

Do you write down your dreams and act on the wisdom you gain from them?			
Are you open-minded?			
Do you trust the process (versus avoiding the unknown)?			
SCORE			

Give yourself 2 points for every Yes, 1 point for every Somewhat, and 0 points for No.

Scale: 4-12 points: Strong need for sixth chakra balancing
13-20 points: Some sixth chakra balancing needed
21-28 points: Congratulations! The sixth chakra of your business is well-balanced.

Questions for Further Exploration

1. When have you used your instincts or intuition in your business? Do you listen and take action based on that information? What happens when you do? What happens when you don't?

2. In what situations do you overthink or overintellectualize? What happens when you do?

3. Where do you sabotage yourself and your business over and over again? List as many examples as you can think of.

4. What are your daydreams about your business?

5. How do you visualize your business? How do you see your business today, one year from now, five years, ten years, etc.?

6. Think of an example of when you have been open-minded. In what situations do you listen to other points of view when making choices and decisions?

7. How do you think others see your business?

8. What dreams do you remember? Write them down in the present tense, if you haven't already. Describe them fully, vividly, and in color.

9. What have you learned about yourself and your business from your dreams?

10. Where do you have controlling tendencies? How does this serve you?

11. How do you ask for guidance in your business, and from whom? People, spiritual guides, angels, ancestors, etc.? Do you feel you receive help?

Ways to Balance Your Sixth Chakra

᨞ Business

- ❏ Do positive visualizations about your business daily.
- ❏ Practice pausing and centering before making decisions.
- ❏ Pause and note how you receive intuitive information and take action based on it.
- ❏ Practice using a balance of rational-analytic and creative-intuitive thinking in your decision-making.
- ❏ Invite other team members and stakeholders into your decision-making.
- ❏ Practice noticing signs and symbols in your daily life and at work. Take action based on them.
- ❏ Practice pausing before entering meetings to receive psychic information.
- ❏ Host outdoor evening team or customer appreciation gatherings or an open house.
- ❏ Evaluate the lighting in your workplace. Replace fluorescent lighting with full-spectrum lighting.
- ❏ Choose paint, flooring, carpeting, artwork, and furniture that will brighten your workspace and create beauty.
- ❏ Use floor and table lamps that will enhance the feel of your environment.

᨞ Body

- ❏ Massage between your eyebrows.
- ❏ Drop into your body through meditation or imagination.
- ❏ Engage in noncompetitive exercise.
- ❏ Do Yantra yoga.
- ❏ Participate in craniosacral body work.
- ❏ Fast for a day.
- ❏ Do a cleansing diet for a month.

❑ Diffuse or wear the following essential oils. For headaches: peppermint, eucalyptus, lavender, rosemary. For focus and memory: focus blend, peppermint.

✍ Emotions

❑ Write down smells, sensations, inner knowing, feelings, and hunches.
❑ Do EFT (Emotional Freedom Technique – also known as tapping).
❑ Create an energy bubble before engaging with challenging people or large groups.
❑ Practice a creative art.
❑ Use your imagination or daydream.
❑ Watch soul-inspiring films.
❑ Create a meditation garden.
❑ Present yourself as a work of art through dress, makeup, etc.
❑ Diffuse or wear the following essential oils to reduce overthinking: sandalwood, myrrh, wild orange, ylang-ylang.

✍ Energy

❑ Listen to guided meditations or visualizations.
❑ Journal your dreams or do other kinds of dream work.
❑ Work with a professional hypnotist.
❑ Create a daily energy bubble around yourself.
❑ Pull tarot or oracle cards daily.
❑ Get your astrological chart done.
❑ Study numerology or sacred geometry.
❑ Carry or wear lapis lazuli.
❑ Wear indigo blue.
❑ Spend some time outside at night under the moon and stars.
❑ Diffuse or wear the following essential oils to create clarity: clary sage, coriander, lemongrass.

✍ Affirmations for the Sixth Chakra

❑ I am intuitive.
❑ I trust my intuition.
❑ It is safe to follow my inner guidance.

❑ I am clear.

❑ My thoughts are calm.

❑ I remember my dreams.

❑ I am creative.

❑ I hear and follow my soul voice.

❑ I see with a whole new level of awareness.

❑ I understand with a deeper level of inner knowing.

❑ I imagine... (a successful business with loads of customers, my best path forward, etc.)

Guided Journey: Moon Pool

The moon governs your intuition. It's a representation of serenity, knowledge, and understanding. It is the guardian of the unconscious and represents inner illumination, divine knowledge, and wisdom. When you seek the moon's energy, you seek to deepen your intuitive understanding of the world and the larger Universe. You access this realm through your imagination, dreams, and symbols.

Imagine it is the edge of night. You sit on the beach watching an enormous pale moon rise in the indigo sky over the dark ocean. Each moment, a star blinks into view. You settle into the warm sand and sit for some time just listening to the rhythmic sounds of the waves hitting the beach while watching the celestial show.

After what seems like a long time, you awaken from your trance. You notice the moon is high in the sky now, and the stars create a net of lights reminiscent of a spider web covering the Universe. You seek where the dark violet of the sky meets the indigo ocean. A faint light moves toward you over the waves. As it gets closer, you see there is a lantern attached to the bow of a sailing ship. A beautiful carved bust of a woman who seems strangely familiar adorns the bow holding a lantern in one hand. The ship sails right up to the shore and lowers a gangplank onto the beach.

A stately woman with an elaborate headdress and long, flowing indigo robe walks down the gangplank. A crescent moon tattoo shines between her brows. Her head is haloed by the full moon wherever she moves, and stars illuminate her hair. What intuitions do you have about this woman?

Effortlessly, she glides over the sand to where you are now standing. She gently gazes into your eyes and then into your soul. Receive her gaze and feel her depth of understanding about you.

She is the Moon Priestess, a seer and a Dreamweaver. She invites you to board the sailing ship and take a trip to Moon Island, where you will connect more deeply to your own special kind of intelligence, intuition, and understanding of the greater Universe. The Moon Priestess hooks arms with you and smiles. Your heart expands with warmth and courage.

You find yourself on board the ship. Enormous white sails billow outward, and the ship eases back into the expansive ocean. You have free reign on this vessel. Explore it as much as you want. What draws your attention? Spend time wandering about allowing your awareness to expand into the night and throughout the ship. As you do, notice what comes to mind. What information do you hear, what notions come to mind, what feelings do you perceive?

After a time, the Moon Priestess finds you. You have arrived at Moon Island. You see the shadow of the island bathed in moonlight. The gangplank lowers, and the two of you disembark onto the island. Take in the sights, sounds, and smells of this place.

There is a path that leads to the heart of the island. You and the Moon Priestess walk this path together. What does it look like? How does it differ from other paths you have walked? How is it the same? Along the path are symbols that mark your journey to your inner knowing and greater understanding. What symbols do you see?

The Moon Priestess stops. Stretching before you lies a crescent-moon-shaped pool. This is a place of initiation. Those who enter this pool release blocks in their third eye chakra, opening up intuition, clear seeing, full imagination, and inner sensing. Take a moment to set your intentions. What do you need to release? What do you need to embrace?

The Moon Priestess invites you to step into the pool. She follows you in. She asks you to trust her. What does your intuition tell you?

She stands behind you and asks you to relax your body into her arms. She lovingly lowers you onto your back in the pool. Your body is completely supported by the waters of intuition and dreams. You float effortlessly. Directly above you, you see the full moon. Its magical light is reflected in the water all around you.

As you float in the moonlight, you feel a new sense of clarity. What do you need to do to balance your third eye chakra? How is your inner dreamer and psychic awareness present in your business?

You feel intense energy swirling around you. It enters your body and surges through you, creating a whole new sense of clarity. What new insights do you receive?

The Moon Priestess assists you out of the water and drapes an indigo robe about your shoulders. Your new status is reflected in the water. A crescent moon tattoo shimmers between your eyebrows. You are now a Moon Priestess and marked as a psychic, seer, and Dreamweaver. The bright energy of the full moon pulses throughout your body. Take your new clarity, understanding, and knowing into the world, and use it in your life and business.

The ship's captain comes and says it is time to return to the mainland. The Moon Priestess says she will remain on the island, that you are ready to walk your new path, but that she is ever present in your life. You always have her guidance, and she will always be there for you. It's time you take your leave. In what manner do you say good-bye?

You return to the sailing ship, and it sets sail for the mainland. You notice the sky getting lighter as you approach the shore. Dawn is breaking. The ship anchors, and you walk down the gangplank. Your feet touch the earth, and the tattoo between your eyebrows tingles with a new clarity and understanding. At the ringing of the chimes, you will return to ordinary reality.

Notes

✑ **Notes** ✑

ᏬᏇᏬ CHAPTER 9 ᏇᏬᏇᏬ

Seventh Chakra: The Spiral Dance

Be the change you wish to see in the world.
Mahatmah Gandhi

*The Law of Divine Compensation posits that this
is a self-organizing and self-correcting Universe: the
embryo becomes a baby, the bud becomes a blossom,
the acorn becomes an oak tree. Clearly, there is
some invisible force that is moving every aspect
of reality to its next best expression.*
Marianne Williamson

CHAKRA 7 QUICK REFERENCE GUIDE

SEVENTH CHAKRA	CORRELATIONS
Sanskrit Name	Sahasrara
Meaning	Thousandfold
Location	Top of the head, cerebral cortex
In the Body Governs	Brain stem, spinal cord, and nervous system
Endocrine Gland	Pineal
Imbalances	Depression, headaches, mental disorders, scalp problems, sleep disorders; live in your head; know it all; holier-than-thou attitude; intellectualism; lack of faith in a higher power, the world, and others; spacedout, detached; can't think for yourself; narrow-mindedness and rigid belief system; choose to be ignorant
Energetic Goals	Spiritual connection, consciousness, understanding, all-knowing; love for all; desire to live more authentically; fully embracing your divine purpose; overcome objections to your chosen path and walk it no matter what others say
Rights	I know, I understand, I am aware
Color	Violet
Food	Fasting
Element	Thought
Stones	Amethyst
Animal	Egg

Archetype	Sage or wise woman
Plant	Lotus flower
Music	Musical note B
Essential Oil	Lavender, frankincense

The spiral has been a symbol of the universal dance in many cultures for millennia, and it captures the essence of the seventh chakra goal for spiritual connection. As a spiritual being in human form, you have a spiritual Source at your soul center from which you spiral out into the world.

According to tantric tradition, a spiral of dormant Kundalini energy lies coiled like a snake at the base of your spine (first chakra). When awakened, it spirals upward, gathering the energy of each chakra, and ultimately leads to an expanded state of consciousness called Kundalini awakening. The seventh chakra is the doorway connecting your spiraling Kundalini energy with your spiritual Source.

The Latin root *spir*, means to "breathe". It is used in words like *inspire*, *aspire*, *spirit*, and of course *spiral*. The spiral has been used in many cultures as a symbol of divine creation and destruction. It encompasses expansion and contraction, winding and unwinding, birth and death.

The labyrinth is an example of the spiral used as a tool for meditation. The process entails staying mentally present as you walk into the labyrinth and back out again, reflecting upon the spiraling nature of the human dance. You may pause in the center of the labyrinth to engage in further meditation. You may walk it faster or slower. You may carefully walk between the lines of the labyrinth, or you may step on the lines purposely or accidentally.

There is no right or wrong way to walk the labyrinth. You go spiritually inward during your walk and return with new insights and wisdom. Regardless of whether you are walking towards the center of the spiral or back out, you have gained knowledge that will help you move forward in your life and business.

When you experience challenges, obstacles, or hardship, there may be times you feel the need to move inward to re-establish your spiritual center. When that happens, it sometimes feels like you are going backwards in life or in your business. But you are actually spiraling towards your spiritual center and gaining another opportunity for soul growth. When you are ready, you will spiral out into the world again – with greater understanding.

Chop Wood, Carry Water

There is a Zen quote, "Before enlightenment, chop wood, carry water. After enlightenment, chop wood, carry water." The spiral dance embraces the spiritual nature of life and business while remaining grounded in everyday tasks. Sometimes there is a misunderstanding that spirituality is separate from real life and especially real business. However, it is only with the help of your spiritual Source that you can truly embrace your soul-purpose and walk your higher business path.

When you seek to discover the soul-purpose of your business, you begin to shift into your crown chakra. Here you experience your own divinity. As you go deeper into your spiritual Source and let go of the false self, your true self emerges. By combining your spiritual connection with your business, you embrace your higher social and ethical purpose in the world.

Even when the inner mob of your small-self is chattering in your head, you will be able to stand in your center and act from a place of faith to accomplish something much bigger than yourself. With trust, you let go of false paths and overcome the objections of critics to walk a more consciously authentic business path.

This is where you unite your seventh chakra with the energies of your other chakras to reach your highest business goals for the greatest good of all. Each chakra brings essential energy to the process. Chakra one builds your foundation, chakra two draws on your passions, chakra three powers your mindful work, chakra four bases you in heart-centered purpose, chakra five supports your authentic communication, chakra six taps into your intuition, and chakra seven connects you with your divine consciousness. Spiral into your spiritual Source and move back out into the world enlightened, ready to "chop wood and carry water."

Spiral Dance Mandala

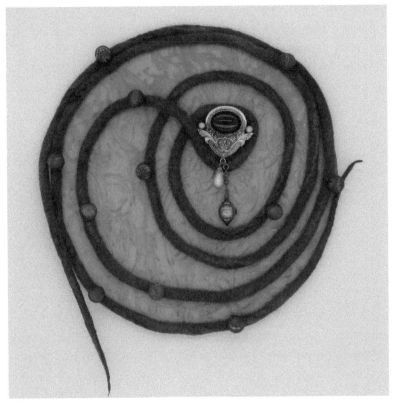

Use a template to draw a circle on a blank piece of paper or cardboard. A paper plate, pie tin, or pizza stone will do nicely, depending on how big you want your circle. Cut out the paper circle with scissors or a utility knife if using cardboard. Fill the circle with a violet purple color using a pen, pencil, paint, or marker. This represents your seventh chakra. Draw, paint, or glue images and symbols within the circle that capture your spiral dance in your business. How have you spiraled into your spiritual Source and out into the world? Think about how your thoughts helped you create your spiral dance and allow that to inform your creative process.

You may wish to use pictures from magazines or found objects from nature or other sources such as leaves, feathers, seeds, buttons, ribbon, glitter, etc. Use one or more colors. The cardboard works best if you plan on gluing heavier objects on your mandala. Let go of the VOJ (Voice of Judgment) and allow yourself free rein. This is not supposed to be a great work of art, just an opportunity for you to spiral into your Source and back out again.

Once you are done, write about your mandala in the Notes section of this chapter. Allow yourself the freedom to write whatever comes to you. Write faster than you can think. Let your hand write the words, instead of your conscious mind. Pay no attention to grammar, punctuation, or spelling, and don't worry about whether it makes sense or not. Continue writing about your mandala until you feel you have completed your thoughts. Then review what you have written.

What knowledge, understanding, awareness, and spiritual connection do you gain from your mandala? How does this apply to your life and business at this time? How will you integrate your thoughts? Keep this information handy for use in the Taking Action section of this chapter.

The Cosmic Egg

Within the spiraling energy of the Universe is the cosmic egg. The egg is the animal symbol for the seventh chakra. The cosmic egg represents new beginnings, potential, limitlessness, purity, and ascension. In some cultures, it is considered the womb of creation from which the world is born. In other cultures, it represents divine birth or rebirth.

As a symbol for your business, the cosmic egg is a reminder of infinite becoming. When you enter into the potential of the universal energies, the possibilities are limitless. All you have to have is faith. Faith! It's so simple to say and oh so hard to do at times. What do you do when obstacles are the theme of the day, week, month, year? What are your thoughts?

It is common for the inner mob to get triggered and start a negative thought spiral that moves out into your life and business to create more obstacles and problems. Like a tornado, it creates a path of destruction and chaos.

Thought is the seventh chakra element and is closely aligned with the cosmic egg symbol of creation. Thought energy vibrates at a high rate and can't be seen with the naked eye, yet form follows thought. This is understood at the spiritual level as well, so much so that in many creation myths, the world is a divine thought that becomes form. Similarly, your thoughts are divinely powerful and can limit or expand your horizons.

How can you incubate positive thoughts so that your cosmic egg (aka your business) hatches in full glory? Some of this requires retraining your brain.

Your brain is wired to be vigilant about anything that might be a threat to you. This is mostly a good thing. Because of this predisposition, you quickly learn not to cross the street without looking, to drive safely, to steer clear of people and situations that could be harmful. The challenge becomes releasing the subconscious thoughts that no longer serve you. For instance, as a child you may have grown up in a family where there was scarcity. Perhaps there was never enough money, and you didn't have the things that other kids did like nice clothes. Maybe you were on the subsidized lunch program. Over time, this experience became part of your internalized truth.

When you are an adult, your subconscious mind unknowingly continues to nurture thoughts of scarcity that show up in your life and business. You continually put these thoughts into the Universe. As a result, you may be struggling to attract the income you would like into your business.

So, how do you change this? You are already doing some of the work needed by completing the exercises in this book. Doing the guided journeys, creating mandalas, journaling, taking action to balance your chakras, creating a Manifestation Board, saying affirmations, making goals, writing your vision, mission, and core values statement – all of these things help you create new neural pathways in your brain, new pathways of positive thought!

Equally important in creating positive thoughts is catching yourself in the act of a negative one. You can't reverse negative thoughts without first becoming aware of them. But, how do you do that? This is where you crack the cosmic egg! The cosmic egg is filled with infinite potential. If your egg is filled with thoughts of what you don't want, guess what? You will attract exactly that. This means you need to become aware of your negative thought patterns. You need to catch yourself thinking negatively so you can begin creating a new mind-set.

Form Follows Thought

Fear is one of the most significant indicators you are operating from negative thoughts – fear of failure, fear of repercussions from your actions, fear of judgment, fear of poor performance, to name a few. When you feel stressed due to fear, it's time to look at your thinking.

Other indicators are harsh judgments about yourself or others. You may be hypercritical of your boss, team members, or customers. You may be plagued by doubts – doubts about your abilities, commitments (yours and those of others), the viability of your business. Or you may worry endlessly about things over which you have little or no control like the economy or the political landscape.

Mind you, there are real situations where it is reasonable to feel fear, be doubtful, worry, and use your judgment. Becoming mindful of when negative thoughts are present will give you a chance to evaluate whether they are a result of pre-programming or a reasonable reaction to what is happening. If they are reasonable, then you can ask your Higher Power to help you create the positive energy to attract what you need to best respond.

The trick is to distinguish between reasonable and pre-programmed negative thoughts. How many times have you thought you didn't have enough money? I have countless times! And the more I think it, the more likely it is to become my reality.

Your mind can be very tricky because habitual negative thoughts can creep in without your awareness. Practice catching yourself in negative thoughts. Then use your rational brain to help you evaluate your thoughts. Is it a pre-programmed negative thought or a situation where you truly need help from your Higher Power? Ask yourself, what would your boss, colleague, team, or customer think about your negative thought? Tease out your typical mind-set and reshape it into positive possibilities.

For example, imagine that your business computers are five years old. You may be feeling stressed out because you rely heavily on computers in your business. You tell an employee, "I don't know what we're going to do. We can't afford to upgrade our computers, and these are nearly obsolete." Evaluate your statement. Do you always feel like there will never be enough money to accomplish the things you need to do? Is it really true? Is there another way to think about it? Ask your team what they think. Perhaps they have a different perspective.

Even if there is real financial stress, the heavy negative energy associated with your thoughts will make it challenging to attract new computers into your business. To shift that, start by creating an affirmation that will offset the negative thoughts. "My business brings in plenty of money to buy the computers we need." Say it three times. This does two things. First of all, it helps retrain your brain and makes new neural pathways that help you believe that you have plenty of money. Second, it counters the negative energy your scarcity thoughts created. Remember, form follows thought.

The next step to creating a new mind-set is to set your intentions for what you want. "We will have the money to buy computers in December of next year." You may not know exactly how it will happen, and that is fine. Put the new computers in your goals. Get specific about model, price, speed, etc. Get a picture of the computers that you want and put it on your Manifestation Board as part of your "heart's desires." At least twice daily (morning and evening), restate your affirmation while looking at your Manifestation Board. Again, this will retrain your brain with new positive thoughts.

Your mind doesn't differentiate between what you imagine and what is real. That is why star athletes will imagine winning over and over again.

It's best if you can bring all your senses into the process of retraining your brain – think the new reality, say it out loud, see a picture of it, imagine how it smells, sounds, and feels. Your brain won't know the difference between your old reality and that which you are "imagining." It will begin to believe the new reality. The internal reality then becomes the external reality because form follows thought.

Your thoughts are limitless, and your ability to create is also limitless. Within you lies the energy of the cosmic egg, waiting to birth new life into your business and life.

A Star is Born

Speaking of cosmic energy, did you know that you and everything else in the Universe is made from stardust? In their book *Living with the Stars*, astrophysicist Karel Schrijver and Stanford University professor of pathology Iris Schrijver write that stardust floats through our bodies. They further state that the majority of atoms in your body were created inside stars when the Universe came into existence billions of years ago. After the Big Bang (merely hundreds of thousands of years ago), gravity pulled the burnt star embers together to form the earth and eventually you. How about that for a connection with the Universe?

The Universe is ever-expanding, birthing new galaxies and stars all the time. This same potential lies within you. For example, it is well known that countless cells in your body die and regenerate several times in your lifetime. You actually re-birth much of your physical self over time.

You also have the infinite ability to re-birth and co-create your outer reality – like your business. As you work to create a purpose-driven business, you spiral deeper into your spiritual Source and tap into the innate universal energies that lie within the embers of your cosmic stardust. You then bring that inspiration and energy into form in the real world. Through this spiral dance, you co-create and re-birth your business with the Universe. Just as the Universe is ever-expanding, your spiritual connection and soul-consciousness are ever-expanding to help you create the best business ever. You truly are the star of your reality!

Clearing Space

There may be times your personal solar system feels overcrowded. Perhaps, you have too many planets in orbit to effectively keep them all spinning. Or maybe new galaxies are being born, and they feel a bit volatile and unstable. You end up feeling overwhelmed and realize you have lost your spiritual Source – your center.

One of the biggest issues in modern society is a lack of focus. You get buzzed every time you receive an email, are dinged by a text, get chimed by a post on Facebook you are following. With the globalization of the economy, a 24-hour business day is not uncommon. With all this going on, in addition to keeping up with the demands of your business and personal life, it's no wonder it feels chaotic. Indeed, you may end up realizing that someone else is creating your reality – not you.

While the Universe was reportedly created in chaos, it is not the best model for your life and business. But how do you keep pace with your ever-expanding Universe? By clearing space. Have you ever organized your closet? If you are like me, I have to pull everything out and then go through the agonizing process of determining what I need to keep and what I need to let go. This can be a challenge for me because I really like clothes and shoes! But, since I have no plans to build a new closet, I've ultimately got to get rid of some things. I have to get real with myself about how the things in my closet are going to serve me. Like that beautiful cashmere sweater I bought and used to wear all the time. It's in great shape and has a lot of life left in it, but I haven't worn it in two years. Hmmm, I probably need to donate it. Your life and business are full of metaphorical cashmere sweaters that may be costing you in terms of time, energy, or money. They may still be useful in some way, but they aren't really serving you anymore.

There are plenty of books available that give advice on how to better organize, better manage your time, and better prioritize tasks, but I am more interested in helping you really narrow down what is (and isn't) indispensable in your life and business right now. In his book *Essentialism*, Greg McKeown promotes creating a "life by design." This entails letting go of things that are nonessential. Because you are living in a culture that encourages clutter, it is more important than ever to determine what is essential to you and to the success of your business (and what is not).

Are you feeling overwhelmed and scattered? It's time to clear some space! Energetically, when you are overburdened, you won't be able to focus your thoughts and actions to manifest the success you want. Your message to the Universe gets garbled because there is no clear signal about what is important to you.

Are there people, things, ideas, commitments, or projects in your life or business that you need to let go of? Taking a critical look at what you need to clear out of your life and business requires that you become aware of why you are holding on to them in the first place.

Do you keep people and things in your life out of feelings of guilt, a sense of duty, hope for a change in external circumstances, or other emotional attachments? We all do at times. Holding onto people and things that anchor you in a past that no longer reflects who you are and where you are going will burden you and keep you energetically stuck.

Being overly busy or distracted by people and/or things keeps you separated from your spiritual Source. Pray to your Higher Power and ask what you need to let go of at this time. There is no special way of doing this. It can be formal or a simple request. Then listen for the answer and know that Spirit has your back.

Where is there clutter? Perhaps you want to clear that closet that seems to gather everything that you have no other place for. Or maybe it's an attic, a basement, under the beds, in cabinets, old files in banker's boxes, etc.

Look at your relationships. Are there people with whom you are spending time who are interfering with your progress personally or professionally? Maybe you are hanging out with some negative people who sap your time and energy. Do you need to spend less time or no time with these people?

What about your commitments? Have you filled your calendar with too many commitments that no longer feed your soul? Perhaps you are on too many boards or committees, or maybe you say yes when you really mean no.

Take an unflinching look at your home, office, relationships, and commitments. Where are you so focused on external things that you have no time to spiral inside and connect with your spiritual Source? Pick one area that you think you need to clear the most and begin the process of elimination. Ask yourself what is truly essential. What is nonessential?

Once you have determined what you need to release, a powerful ritual can be to write down a list of the things, people, and/or commitments you wish to release and then burn or bury your list. This will further release that stagnant energy and signal the Universe that you are ready to let go of old energy so that fresh energy can come in. It is especially powerful to do a ritual energy release during a full moon.

Tossing the Stones[v]

Another ritual to help you release what you no longer need is to metaphorically toss away the burden of the stones you have been slowly gathering on your journey. You may wish to invite others to join you in this process.

1. Find a quiet, private space and place a small blanket, tablecloth, or scarf in in the center to make a floor altar. You may want to include flowers or important power objects.

2. Gather a pile of stones and place them at the center as well – two per person.

3. Place an open basket or other nonbreakable container next to the stones.

4. Bring your spiritual Source into the confidential, sacred space you've created. For example, you may recite a small prayer or poem or do a quiet meditation to invite your spiritual Source into the space.

5. Sit in a relaxed state and imagine the following (if desired, you can record this and play it back during the ceremony).

> *You are walking on a dirt path. It is a lovely day. There is a slight breeze, and the sun is warm. You are calm and rested. You carry an empty backpack on your back. As you walk, you notice there are stones along the path. Some lie among the wildflowers on both sides of the path, but others rest in the middle where you are walking. You stop and pick up one of the stones. Notice the size, color, texture, and weight. You decide to keep it and put it in your backpack.*
>
> *You continue your walk. But you are having trouble focusing on the beautiful day and scenery. Instead, you are distracted by all the stones on your path. You pick up several more and put them in your backpack. Notice the size, color, texture, and weight of each stone.*
>
> *Your backpack is feeling very heavy from the weight of the stones. The path has taken you into a dense forest. You are feeling tired, tense and irritable. Where do you feel this most in your body? Where do you feel this most in your soul?*
>
> *You are just about ready to stop following your path, when you hear the sound of a waterfall up ahead. You follow the sound to a clearing where, at the bottom of a steep embankment, you see a waterfall and a large, clear pool of water. You stand at the edge of the pool, hot and tired, feeling a deep desire to descend into the water. However, you can't climb down safely with a heavy pack of stones on your back.*
>
> *You take off your heavy pack and unpack the stones you've*

gathered along your walk. Do you want to continue to carry these stones on your current path? Your answer is no. Pick up the stones and toss them, one by one, over the steep embankment into the far end of the pool.

Feeling greatly relieved, you realize that you no longer need your backpack since you aren't carrying the stones. So you leave it behind and climb down the embankment. You can see the stones you threw, lying on the bottom of the far end of the pool. You turn in the opposite direction and head to the waterfall. There you take off your clothes and immerse yourself in the mildly cool water. You are relaxed and feel completely released from the burden of the stones.

When you feel refreshed, you redress and return along the path to your home. You no longer pick up the stones along the path. You are free!

Very slowly bring your awareness back to the present. Once you are fully back, choose the top two burdens you need to release. Next choose two stones and toss them in the basket while naming what you are releasing.

Make the task of clearing what you released another ritual. You may only have a few minutes a day or maybe you have hours, but make each task a sacred act. Before you engage in it, you may wish to say a prayer, light a candle, burn incense, or diffuse clary sage or lavender essential oils to set the stage for a ritual act versus just another task. Whatever tasks you carry out, do them with conscious, sacred intention. After all, you are clearing sacred space for Spirit to enter. It may take hours, days, weeks or months to fully clear what you need to. Starting is the hard part. Ask Spirit for the help you need to accomplish your tasks. You may want to put it on your calendar to help hold yourself accountable, or engage a friend, colleague, or coach as an accountability partner.

I promise, once you are done clearing, you will feel great! Celebrate! Give thanks! You have just opened up a big energetic door to your spiritual Source.

Altar Your Reality

In some parts of the world, it is common for there to be small sacred altars throughout the home and/or workplace. An altar is a reminder that all that you do is sacred, whether at home, at work, or in the community. I have one in a corner of my home office where I do my morning meditation. It reminds me that I am in service to something bigger than myself and that I have spiritual help.

My altar contains pendulums, chakra stones, healing crystals, a little hand-felted goddess, and a Goddess Box. Each of these items reminds me of my Higher Power – a universal energy greater than myself. I know I have guides to help me, and I don't have to figure it all out on my own.

Altars can be very simple. If you have a desk where you routinely work, you may consider using a corner of it as an altar by placing a candle, special photos, a piece of art, or a healing stone on it. A small table or corner cabinet will also house an altar nicely.

The key is to create a spiritual space that is meaningful to you. You may decide that somewhere out in nature provides a better spiritual space for you. Nature may be your cathedral where you take a contemplative walk. You may have a book nook where you meditate and write in your journal. Perhaps you have a few cushions and pillows on the floor in a cozy corner where you listen to guided meditations or meditative music. Try singing, chanting, and dancing alone or with others in a common room.

What feels natural to you? You may have more than one place (some inside, some outside) where you commune with your Higher Power. Consider how much privacy you need and how easily you get distracted by things or noise. The most important thing is to set aside a time and space to do your spiritual contemplation.

Communing with your Higher Power is an important piece of tapping into the energy of your seventh chakra on your way to spiritual wholeness. Daily is best, but several times a week is great. From my own experience, it becomes very apparent when I have not been doing my spiritual practice. My inner mob gets very noisy, and I am more likely to make decisions from an emotional place rather than a neutral, spiritually centered place.

When you operate your business from your inner divine, you also become a portal for your team to step into their inner divine and show up ready for service to others for the highest good of all.

Making a God/dess Box

Even though I try to work mostly from a spiritual place, there are times my small-self gets triggered. I have obsessed about conversations in which I felt personally attacked, endlessly thinking about what I wish I had said. There have been times I've sent an email in anger in a less than god/dess-like way, and then I've needed to figure out a way to apologize and shift the energy.

That is when my God/dess Box comes in handy. A Goddess (or God) Box is a lidded box or container in which you can put written messages.

You may wish to decorate one yourself, or you may have the perfect container already in mind.

Write down your worries, anger, angst, confusion about people and issues that you have no control over, or situations where you haven't quite figured out how to change yourself and your energy. And then put them in your God/dess Box.

By placing your concerns there, you are ritually releasing them. You are letting go and letting God/dess handle them. By doing so, you no longer need to carry the burden of what you can't or don't know how to change at this time. Often your challenges aren't totally in your control anyway. You can only change your own energy, mind-set, and behaviors, and not those of others.

While you are on your soul-journey, you are in process. You rely on spiritual support to help you change your personal and professional perspectives, behaviors, and energy. The messages you put in your God/dess Box are individual prayers, direct links to your Higher Power who will help you find solutions in a more holistic way than you could ever conceive.

Expect the Unexpected

Relying on your Higher Power to find the best solutions is often a challenge, because it means you have to surrender control. It requires you to give up expectations of how something is going to look exactly and *trust*. That doesn't mean throw your plan out the window. It does mean your plan may manifest in unexpected ways. The key is to trust that, when it manifests differently, it will be even better than you ever imagined.

There is a delicate balance between setting intentions, planning, and taking action. Trying to force something to happen almost never works. Holding onto an idea, expectation, or outcome too tightly is a surefire way to shut down the energy needed to allow Spirit to work out a solution for your highest good and the highest good of all.

For example, for the previous seven years, as of the writing of this book, I dreamed of having an office-studio space where I could see clients, do Reiki, have small classes, write, and create art. After discussing it with many people, I determined I needed a large space that was centrally located with easy access for my clients. Sounds like a good idea, right?

I first rented a large, shared studio in a converted mill with two other women. It was reasonably priced and inviting. The only problem was that it was an open floor plan, so I had to schedule my client and class times when others weren't there. That proved to be challenging. After three years, I let go of that space.

I then used the upper story of the building of the local food store we owned. That worked for a couple of years, until we sold the building. Next, I subleased a beautiful little office for a couple of years, which was perfect for seeing clients but had limited space for classes or anything else.

It finally dawned on me that I was operating out of a limiting belief that I had to have a space that was convenient for everyone – that no one would be willing to travel to my home office. Talk about a self-value issue. Once I released that thought, I was able to see the potential of creating the space I wanted at my house. I updated the front door so clients could come in a separate entrance. I now see coaching clients, and Reiki clients, have classes, write, and make art in my beautiful, tax-deductible home office-studio.

It was only after I made the switch that I remembered that it was my original heart's desire to see clients and have classes in a home office-studio. But first I had to release my self-limiting beliefs and the opinions of others. Good thing Spirit was listening. If I had trusted Spirit more, I would have saved myself a lot of time, effort, and money.

How are you limiting yourself? Where are you trying to force an outcome and keep bumping up against repeated obstacles? Have there been opportunities that presented themselves, but you opted out because you had your plans already all laid out?

Every step of your business journey requires you to be present in the now. Only then can you follow the yesses. Following the yesses means stepping through the open doors on your path that will take you closer to your goals. They may or may not be doors you originally conceived of opening. These are doors that your Higher Power opens for you, and all you have to do is say yes and step through.

Sometimes a door may be open only a crack or appear slightly ajar rather than wide open. Then what? Do you peek through the door and try to determine what's on the other side before you walk through? What unexpected people, events, or opportunities lie on the other side? Are you hindered by your fear of the unknown? Do you wait for it to open wide or walk through in spite of your incomplete view?

Every door (whether it is wide open or just ajar) gives you an opportunity to receive universal energy – to move in a direction you hadn't planned. Of course not every open door is a universal portal to your highest goals.

This is where you have to spiral in and sit in your spiritual center. Ask your Higher Power, "Is this for my highest good, the highest good of my loved ones, the highest good of my business, the highest good of all?"

Use the tools discussed in Chapter 8 to tap into your psychic intuition, which is connected to your Higher Power, to help you get to the heart of the matter. Also, determine if a new door is essential or nonessential. If it is essential, is there something nonessential that needs to be cleared out to make space?

When you open up your seventh chakra energy, your greatest potential opens up. Notice how you spiritually show up in your personal and professional life. Is your starlight shining in a way that will bring you success and honor your soul and the soul-purpose of your business?

Take a moment to sit in meditation and spiral inside. Then, in the Notes section, write a prayer to your Higher Power and ask how you can co-create your business in a way that connects you with its soul-purpose. Read what you have written. Make this prayer a part of a daily spiritual practice. Watch as Spirit unfolds the wrinkles of the Universe and your true soul path appears.

Putting It Into Practice

It's Monday morning, and it is very quiet at Rainbow Integrated Healthcare. Even though all the team members are there, everyone is silently preparing for the clients who will be arriving in about an hour.

Megan and Valerie are shut up in their respective offices. Meditative music floats from under Megan's door. There is shuffling and quiet cursing coming from Valerie's office.

Megan emerges and proceeds to knock on Valerie's door. Valerie opens it with a scowl on her face. "What do you want?" she asks with open hostility.

"I want to talk to you," Megan answers neutrally.

"Fine!" Valerie responds hotly and slams the door shut.

"I have been praying about our relationship and RIH over the weekend," Megan states simply.

Valerie rolls her eyes.

"I want you to know I think we have something very

unique here that I would love to see come to full fruition. You have a powerful vision, Valerie, one that all the team members believe in. If team members are allowed to use their gifts fully, we can make your vision materialize. If you will relinquish some control to others and start focusing more on the positive things going on here, I truly think we will co-create something better than our wildest imaginings."

Valerie listens silently. Megan continues, "Fear is poisoning the organization. Your fears move energetically into the larger team and are creating a collective energetic shutdown. I think that is why we are running into so many obstacles to attaining our goals."

Megan takes a deep breath and states compassionately, "If things don't change, RIH will not survive. Valerie, I think you might benefit from some coaching to help you work through your negative mind-set and help you tap into your inner Source – your Higher Power. I've been working with a coach, and I'm sure she could help you or refer you to someone who could. I never would have been able to have this kind conversation before I met her."

Valerie slumps in her chair and looks at Megan with tears in her eyes. "I'm just so afraid that people will take advantage of me that I put up a fierce front. I know I'm pushing people away. I saw my father do the same thing at home and in his career. He always said that you can't trust people and that it doesn't matter if people like you. That it is more important to maintain control. I don't know if I can change."

Megan puts her arm around Valerie. "Do you want to keep repeating your current reality? It seems like you are in a lot of personal pain. We are all on a spiritual journey to wholeness. Perhaps we can use RIH as part of our path to get there."

Valerie jumps up, startling Megan. "I've got it! We will make personal growth part of the continuing education goal."

"I love that," Megan replies. "My coach works with organizations using the PeerSpirit Circle Process. I'm sure she would be able to help us gain greater awareness and move us toward a more holistic culture."

"It will be a lot of work," worries Valerie.

"Yes, it will, but it will be worth it." Megan smiles.

When Megan looked to her Higher Power for solutions to the current situation, she was able to approach Valerie with compassion rather than fear. With Spirit's support, she was able to step into her power and take the needed action. She received the right words and energetic approach from her spiritual Source to break through the energetic wall that Valerie had created for herself.

No doubt there is a great deal of work to be done on everyone's part, but using a holistic model to work with the team mentally, physically, spiritually, and energetically will set the stage for growth of cosmic proportions for each person and for RIH as a whole.

Taking Action

Now it's time for you to take action. Carry out the following activities to help you determine what your next steps need to be in order for you to be able to appropriately harness and exercise the seventh chakra power of your business.

1. Take the Chakra Assessment that follows and record your score. Does it indicate a glaring deficit in this chakra or just some tweaking?

2. Answer the Questions for Further Exploration that follows and write down any insights, new ideas, or awareness you may have.

3. Listen to the Wise Sage guided journey on the website and journal about your experience: www.nanettegiacoma.com/OpenForBusinessBook.

4. Review the information and insights you have gathered from this chapter about the seventh chakra.

5. Read Ways to Balance Your Seventh Chakra, which follows, and select which things you want to try or make your own list of ideas.

6. From your list, choose 1-3 things you are going to do.

    a. ___ What action steps will you take?

b.___ Do you need help? What kind of help? From whom?

c.___ When will you start? What is your goal completion date?

d.___ How will you know you have reached your goal?

SEVENTH CHAKRA ASSESSMENT

Seventh Chakra	Yes	No	Somewhat
Do you believe in a Higher Power?			
Do you believe you receive guidance and take action based on spiritual support?			
Are you able to let go of control and let god/dess take the lead?			
Have you experienced miracles in your business?			
Is your business mostly clear of nonessentials?			
Do you think you are fulfilling the higher soul-purpose of your business?			
Do you believe that the positive and negative thoughts you put out in the world come back to you in kind?			
Do you have a spiritual practice (meditation, prayer, yoga, etc.)?			
Are you able to get emotionally neutral for balanced thinking and decision-making?			
Are you mostly able to stay mentally focused when needed?			

Do you model the things in your business you wish to see in the world?			
Are you able to see value in differing belief systems?			
SCORE			

Give yourself 2 points for every Yes, 1 point for every Somewhat, and 0 points for No.

Scale: 4-12 points: Strong need for seventh chakra balancing

13-20 points: Some seventh chakra balancing needed

21-28 points: Congratulations! The seventh chakra of your business is well-balanced.

Questions for Further Exploration

1. How strong is your faith in your business purpose and direction? Explain what faith means to you.

2. What soul crises or faith crises have you overcome in your life or business or are you in the process of overcoming? Explain.

3. What miracles have you witnessed in your business and life?

4. Explain how you are spiritually connected to others.

5. What is your spiritual practice? If none, what would you like to commit to?

6. Describe how you pray and how frequently you pray.

7. What are your beliefs about "The Power of Attraction" that claims that the thoughts we put out in the world come back to us, whether they be positive or negative.

8. What physical or mental issues are you experiencing related to the seventh chakra? Why do you think that is?

Ways to Balance Your Seventh Chakra

∽ Business

❑ Share with your team how you operate your business from a place of higher purpose and authenticity.

❑ Write your personal higher mission statement and how it benefits the world.

- ❏ Imagine daily the business you want; invite stakeholders to participate.
- ❏ Start your day at work with a spiritual practice like meditation or silence.
- ❏ Create a meditation or quiet space at work.
- ❏ Make a small altar in your workspace.
- ❏ Pause and take ten breaths before saying yes to a new commitment or decision.
- ❏ Play baroque (or other alpha wave) music throughout the day for better focus.
- ❏ Sponsor a nonprofit cause and donate food, money, or needed supplies.
- ❏ Incorporate the color violet into your workspace.
- ❏ Diffuse or wear the following essential oils for focus: focus blend, peppermint.

☙ Body

- ❏ Rest on day seven.
- ❏ Enter a sensory deprivation tank and observe your mental processes.
- ❏ Fast or "energize" your food before you eat it with prayer or intentions.
- ❏ Go on a cleansing diet for 30 days.
- ❏ Go on a holistic healing retreat.
- ❏ Take warm cleansing baths with pink Himalayan salt and lavender oil.
- ❏ Practice Jnana yoga.
- ❏ Practice Tai Chi.
- ❏ Practice Qigong.
- ❏ Diffuse or wear the following essential oils for headaches: peppermint, eucalyptus, lavender, rosemary.

☙ Emotions

- ❏ Make a God/dess Box and place your worries and concerns inside.
- ❏ Make a list of negative thoughts and rationally evaluate each one.
- ❏ Hire a spiritual or holistic executive coach.

- ❏ Take a class about other faiths.
- ❏ Read spiritually based books.
- ❏ Take a class on something thought-provoking.
- ❏ Go on a spiritual retreat.
- ❏ Count your breaths when emotionally uncentered.
- ❏ Diffuse or wear the following essential oils to reduce overthinking: sandalwood, myrrh, ylang-ylang.
- ❏ Diffuse or wear the following essential oils for depression: frankincense, wild orange, lemon, lavender, joyful blend.

❧ Energy

- ❏ Pray.
- ❏ Meditate daily.
- ❏ Practice affirmations twice daily.
- ❏ Embark on a pilgrimage.
- ❏ Bless yourself and others daily.
- ❏ Do nothing for a day and spend it in contemplation.
- ❏ Clear space in your life and/or business by getting rid of nonessential things, relationships, and commitments.
- ❏ Wear the color violet.
- ❏ Carry or wear amethyst.
- ❏ Diffuse or wear the following essential oils for spiritual connection: lavender or frankincense.

❧ Affirmations for the Seventh Chakra

- ❏ I know.
- ❏ I understand.
- ❏ I am aware.
- ❏ I am expanded consciousness.
- ❏ I am love.
- ❏ I am light.
- ❏ I am at peace.
- ❏ I trust life.
- ❏ I am connected to all that is.

❑   I am Divine.

❑   I am the change in the world I wish to see.

Guided Journey: Wise Sage

When you seek to discover your essence in life, you begin to shift into your seventh chakra, the crown chakra. Here you experience the Divine. You become one with your inner sage, who is connected to your Higher Power. As you go deeper, you let go of the false self and your true self emerges. This is where your body, mind, and soul unite.

Imagine that you are surrounded by a sea of violets. Their soft fragrance reaches your nose as the delicate purple heads nod in the breeze. Look around. How does the beauty and fragrance affect you? Notice your peace of mind, as you stand engulfed in this violet sea. Beautiful music serenades you from an unknown source, filling you with something that approaches perfection.

Looking up, you see seven rainbows above you. Turn around where you are standing and notice how they arch directly overhead, encompassing you and the field of violets. A thought springs to mind: "I want to touch a rainbow." As soon as you think it, you feel your feet rising off the ground, and the next thing you know, you are standing on air. How is it possible? Do you struggle to make sense of it? What are your thoughts?

You greatly want to reach the rainbow nearest you. You try swimming through the air to the rainbow, but you don't get very far. Next, you try walking there – also unsuccessfully. Then it dawns on you that thought is the element of the seventh chakra. With perfect clarity, you suddenly know that your positive thoughts will take you to a rainbow. With extraordinary focus, reach out with your mind and touch the rainbow nearest you. You instantly find yourself sitting on a rainbow. The other six rainbows create a web of color around you.

Sitting next to you cross-legged is the Wise Sage. What do you notice about this mystical being? The Wise Sage reaches out to you with their mind, and a ribbon of rainbow colors blends into a brilliant white light that flows into your crown chakra and down your body, bathing you in a beautiful glow. How does the world look from within the light? How do you feel? What are your thoughts?

Notice everything you can about this experience.

Without speaking, the Wise Sage lets you know they will guide you on a spiritual journey to your Higher Power. Take a moment to fully absorb that and see if you can sense your connection with your Higher Power. Close your eyes for a moment.

Again, your Wise Sage touches your mind with theirs. You initially feel a sense of serenity that then transforms into expansiveness. You are transported into another dimension, beyond time and space as you know it. When you open your eyes, you find yourself at the center of the Universe. Use all your senses to experience the wonder.

The Wise Sage brings your attention to a spark of light that looks like a tiny star. Sit in the light of this star for a moment. Feel its energy expand into your energy field. Startled, you realize that this tiny star contains your essence. You are made from stardust... the most powerful substance in the Universe. Fully embrace the wisdom and power of your Source.

As you absorb this knowledge about your Source, you feel a tremendous presence. Your Higher Power reveals Itself to you. How do you experience this? As a feeling? A being? An energy?

You are filled to bursting with the deep understanding that you are loved completely; indeed, you are the embodiment of love. You feel an intense stirring in your soul as your Higher Power shares with you your true purpose. What are you are destined to share with the world?

Reflect on your journey up to this point. What do you need to do differently, if anything? Throughout your journey, your Higher Power is always present. Although you may feel separate at times, you too are a divine being, at one with your Higher Power. Consciously unite now with your Higher Power. Imagine yourself merging as one being. Embrace the divinity within you. How do you experience this?

Filled with the wisdom, power, and love of your own divinity, return to the field of violets. Do you experience it differently?

As you pause to reflect, you notice an object on the ground. This object will remind you of your divinity when you are feeling disconnected. What is the object? In whatever manner feels right to you, express your gratitude for your divine connection.

In a few moments, you will return to the present reality. You will feel complete peace and contentment, deep love, and an unwavering sense of connection with your divinity. At the ringing of the chimes, bring your awareness back to ordinary reality.

❧ Notes ❧

❧ Notes ❧

ᥱᑌᡃᠣ CHAPTER 10 ᠥᡃᡑᠣᡅ

Chakra Harmony: Riding the Rainbow

Chakras are the organizational centers for the reception, assimilation and transmission of life-force energy. They are the stepping stones between heaven and earth.

Anodea Judith

Nothing can dim the light that shines from within.

Maya Angelou

In a balanced state, bright rainbow energy consistently courses up and down your chakras, which is then hyperlinked to your life and business. You naturally ride the rainbow energy as it flows in your body, connecting you with the grounded energy of the Earth and the infinite energy of the universe.

But often real life and real business get in the way of a smooth rainbow ride. You may find yourself frequently working on personal and/or professional obstacles. Some legs of your journey may take a week – a month, a year, a lifetime - to complete. Other team members in your business may also have similar work to do.

Most likely you and your business currently have one or more chakras in need of some balancing. Harmonizing and integrating your chakra energy is a journey. Sometimes your chakras and those of your business are clearer, and at other times some may be muddied. A chakra may be under-energized at one point and over-energized at another. Although I have mostly discussed the chakras individually, riding the energy of the rainbow depends upon a clear connection between all of them. When imbalances occur, the flow between the chakras can become blocked and often create obstacles, issues, and illnesses.

Balanced chakras begin with you, whether that is in your life or business. You must take the steps toward wholeness. You may decide to begin by focusing on your physical, emotional, or spiritual self. Or there may be specific areas of your life or business that you need to address first. In some ways, it doesn't really matter how you begin or what approach you take, since it is all energy and will ultimately connect and move into the other areas. For example, if you start to get serious about doing some self-care (a first chakra concern) the corresponding energy in your life and business will be affected. Perhaps you will see that you are better able to curb your operating expenses so that your business is more financially stable (also a first chakra concern).

You recall that imbalances create excessive (overactive) chakras or deficient (underactive) chakras. It isn't uncommon for there to be patterns of imbalances that are connected to one or more chakras.

To help you get a better sense of your personal patterns of imbalance, take a clean sheet of paper and draw seven circles stacked one on top of the other, similar to the chakras as they align with your spine. Make the size of each circle correlate with the imbalance or balance of your in-body chakra. For example, you may see from your notes, assessments, and observations that you have an extremely excessive third chakra. This will be the largest circle in your line. Maybe your sixth chakra is really deficient. This will be the smallest circle in your line. There is no right or wrong way to do this exercise. Just use your own judgment to get a picture of how your chakras line up. Now add some color, using a colored pencil, paint, or marker. Are the chakra colors clear and bright? Do any have a muddier hue?

Now do the same process for your business chakras. Is there a correlation between your personal chakras and your business chakras? Where are the similarities? Where are the differences? Make note of the similarities and differences in the Notes section of this chapter.

Observe whether you show more imbalances in the lower chakras and tend to compensate by mostly utilizing the energy of your upper chakras. Perhaps, you overevaluate things intellectually before acting on them. Overevaluation indicates a sixth chakra excess. You get engrossed in the analysis and forget to access your third chakra energy to take action. Or maybe you voice your opinions without thinking about possible reactions from others. This would indicate an excessive fifth chakra, entirely missing the energetic goal for connection essential to a healthy second chakra.

On the flip side, if you tend towards imbalances in your upper chakras, you may use your lower chakras more. You may have a high need to be financially secure before making changes in your life or business. Your first chakra need for safety and security may keep you focused on maintaining the status quo, whereas tapping into the intuitive wisdom of your sixth chakra would enable you to make needed changes confidently. Or you may value hard work above most everything else and forget the more spiritual aspects of life. In which case, you are overcompensating for your deficient seventh chakra by becoming a workaholic and relying heavily on your excessive third chakra. How does your chakra balance/imbalance pattern show up in your body, life, and business?

Review your individual business chakra assessments and notice if you have more imbalances in the upper or lower chakras or if your imbalances are more isolated. In particular, look hard at one or two chakras where most of your imbalances are. Do they correlate with the chakra circle exercises from above? Jot down your observations in the Notes section of this chapter.

To further help you analyze your business chakra system, there is a chart in the appendixes of this book that summarizes the most common business and professional chakra issues, challenges, and obstacles and tells which chakra they correspond to and whether they indicate deficient or excessive energy in the chakra.

For a more in-depth look at deficient and excessive chakra energy in your personal chakra system, Anodea Judith's book, *Eastern Body Western Mind*, is a great resource.

Let's Get Physical

Since chakra energy initiates in your body, getting into your body is an important way to start harmonizing and integrating your chakras. Yoga is based on the chakra system and is a great way to get chakra energy moving. Tai Chi is also excellent because it practices focused physical movement that amounts to a moving meditation. Focusing on specific chakras while dancing is another terrific practice. For example, the hip and torso movements in belly dancing are fantastic for the second and third chakras. Hand drumming can help you dive down into your first chakra and pull the deep vibrations into your body.

While any type of physical exercise can potentially benefit your chakras, notice if you are really in your body while doing it. If you tend to ignore the messages your body is sending you and live more in your head, it will be especially important to make the effort to get into your body while exercising. Notice what your body is communicating to you while running, strength training, doing the elliptical, riding your bike, etc. Are you overdoing it? Or perhaps you are just going through the motions.

Look at the ways to balance your chakras for the body that have been previously listed, and see if there is something different you might like to try that will shake up the status quo. For instance, I did belly dancing for a time because I knew I had some imbalances in my second chakra. Not only did learning how to gyrate my hips and torso help shake up my second chakra, but because I was learning something new, I found I had to focus on how my body moved and how it felt to move it in a new way. In what new way do you need to move and focus your body?

A Fine Silver Thread

In her book *The Celtic Chakras*, Elen Sentier describes a silver thread connecting the chakras. In the Celtic tradition, the Quicksilver Path begins in the center of the fourth (heart) chakra and spirals through the center of each chakra. From the fourth chakra, your energetic silver thread spirals down through the third chakra, then up through the fifth, down through the second, up through the seventh, and down through the first, before finally entering the sixth chakra.

Quicksilver Path

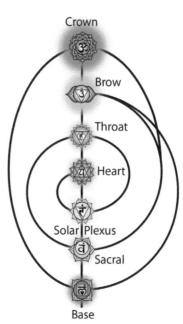

While this is a different experience from that of Kundalini energy snaking its way from the root chakra up through the crown chakra, it is another excellent way to experience chakra energy in your body.

Try using the Celtic spiraling Quicksilver Path to learn more about your chakras. Start by getting into a comfortable position, close your eyes, and take a few calming breaths. Focus on your heart chakra center. Explore the sensations there. Sit with your heart chakra a few moments. What does it have to teach you? Now spiral through the center of each chakra as illustrated, and do the same getting-to-know-you process, ending with your third eye chakra.[vi]

Did you receive any insights or different information using this method?

Energy Management

Riding the rainbow requires that you shift how you are currently managing your energy. Based on the information you have gathered, where are the major imbalances in your body, your life, and your business? Are you becoming more aware of how you might be compensating for some imbalances by using your other chakras?

While I have given you several tools and processes to help you shift your imbalances, you may need some extra help. A good energy healer is worth their weight in gold. Well-known energy healing modalities in the U.S. include Reiki, acupuncture, acupressure, Eden's Energy Medicine, Emotional Freedom Technique (EFT), polarity therapy, pranic healing, and shamanic healing, to name just a few. There are many types of energy healers, and each has something valuable to offer. Use your intuition. Is there one you think would benefit you? If so, give it a try.

Personally, as a Reiki Master, I have used Kundalini and Usui Reiki when coaching clients and have seen how their lives, careers, and businesses have shifted. I worked with one client who was recently divorced and had just received her RN degree. After a false start in one healthcare organization, Nina came to me for coaching and energy work. She was looking for new work that would support her need to be available for her children, earn a wage to buy a new home, and fill her need for purposeful work.

The first thing Nina did was get very clear about her desires using her second and fourth chakra energy. Using her second chakra, she dipped into her feelings and remembered how it felt to do work she liked and felt good about. She then took those feelings and connected them to her heart chakra, whereupon her heart sent her desires out into the quantum field in search of synchronistic events and people.

Nina listed exactly what she wanted in her new work – how much money she wanted to earn, desired schedule, ideal location, work environment, organizational culture, etc. Through this process she engaged her third and fourth chakras' energy. First, she used her third chakra to get clear about her core values as they related to balancing family and work and what type of organization would support her values. Her core values became the basis for her goals. She then engaged the super power inherent in her fourth chakra to set her intentions to attract what she desired.

Next, she kept her own counsel about what was best for her. She didn't listen to others or her inner mob. In fact, she only shared her goals with a few people she knew would support her – no naysayers allowed! Nina combined her first chakra energetic need for safe boundaries with the healthy communication inherent in her fifth chakra to achieve this. To seal the deal, I used Kundalini Reiki to further release any energetic barriers to her success.

Nina was very selective about only applying for work that met her criteria. She further engaged her third chakra energy to stay on her path to reach her goals. After about six months, she found the perfect job, and it paid her more than she had even imagined. And while the location wasn't quite as close as she would have liked, she intuitively knew (sixth chakra) it was the right position. Her guides had obviously come through for her (seventh chakra).

You can see from this example that managing your energy often requires consciously using a combination of chakra techniques and tools, which may include getting help from an energy healer. Often discomfort is an invitation to manage your energy differently – no matter where the discomfort arises. If you are having difficulty overcoming obstacles, tap into your seventh chakra and ask your spirit guides what you are resisting that is preventing you from shifting your energy. Go deeply into your discomfort to learn the truth of what you need to do to ride your rainbow energy.

Riding the Rainbow Mandala

Use a template to draw a circle on a blank piece of paper or cardboard. A paper plate, pie tin, or pizza stone will do nicely, depending on how big you want your circle. Cut out the paper circle with scissors or a utility knife if using cardboard. When the light and colors of the rainbow are blended, they appear white. So fill the circle with a white color using a pen, pencil, paint, or marker. This represents the integration of the chakras. Draw, paint, or glue images and symbols within the circle that capture how you imagine or experience the integration of rainbow energy in your body, life, and business. What does integration look like? How does harmony feel? Allow the Quicksilver Path bodywork you did to inform your process.

You may wish to use pictures from magazines or found objects from nature or other sources such as leaves, feathers, seeds, buttons, ribbon, glitter, etc. Use one or more colors. The cardboard works best if you plan on gluing heavier objects on your mandala. Let go of the VOJ (Voice of Judgment) and allow yourself free rein. This is not supposed to be a great work of art, just an opportunity for you to tap into what the integration and harmony of your chakras look like.

Once you are done, write about your mandala in the Notes section of this chapter. Allow yourself the freedom to write whatever comes to you. Write faster than you can think. Let your hand write the words instead of your conscious mind. Pay no attention to grammar, punctuation, or spelling, and don't worry about whether it makes sense or not. Continue writing about your mandala until you feel you have completed your thoughts. Then review what you have written.

What feelings, thoughts, and sensations came up for you? How does this apply to your life and business at this time?

Not Business as Usual

By now you have a great deal of information! You have done the assessments, created mandalas, listened to the guided journeys, created goals, and completed other exercises in this book. How do you take all this and make real life and real business changes?

Perhaps you got to the end of the chakra seven chapter and realized you need to rethink your goals. Somewhere in the course of this book, you may have had an epiphany and need to rewrite your vision and mission statements. Maybe you are feeling completely overwhelmed at this point and don't know what to focus on first.

If that is the case, review the information that you have gathered throughout this book. In particular, look at your actions and goals at the end of each chakra chapter. Also, look at the pictures of how your chakras line up in terms of excesses and deficiencies. What themes are present? What obstacles, illness, or issues do you currently have? Where are these connected, and how do they show up as recurring themes in your business, life, and body?

It's All in the Cards

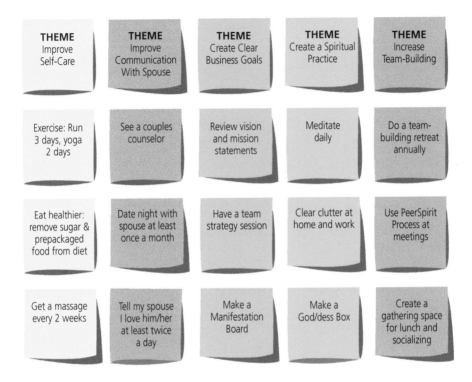

Card sorting is a tool to help you determine themes. (I use sticky notes instead of cards.) For this exercise, you will need a stack of three-by-three-inch sticky notes (bigger if you like to write big). You will also need a blank wall or a large piece of paper (two by three feet).

1. Write each action/goal for working on your chakras on a sticky note. One goal per sticky note.

2. Place your sticky notes on the wall or paper so that you group together actions/goals that are related. You will end up with several vertical columns of sticky notes.

3. Keep sorting until you feel like you have them all placed where they make sense to you. Don't worry if they don't make sense to others. This is your process.

4. If you have a hard time choosing where an action/goal needs to be placed, close your eyes and take a few breaths. Consciously engage your sixth chakra. Let your intuition guide you.

5. Once you have several vertical rows of sticky notes, take a clean sticky note and write a heading/theme for each row. If helpful, you can use different-colored sticky notes or ink to organize your headings/themes.

6. Place each theme at the top of the respective row. Now you have your themes.

7. Next, rank your themes (1 to 10) based on priority, with 1 being your lowest priority and 10 your highest.

8. Look at the top three to five themes.

9. Now consolidate your actions/goals within each theme. There may be similarities.

10. Prioritize the consolidated actions/goals (1 to 10) within each theme.

11. Focus on the top three to five actions/goals from the top three to five themes to get the most significant results.

All aspects of your body, life, and business are connected energetically, even if your top themes seem to be unrelated. So it's possible one of your top themes will focus on a first chakra concern, like self-care and taking good care of your body (body energy). Your next theme may be to work on a fifth chakra issue, like improving communication with your spouse (life energy), and a final theme may be a third chakra need to get clear about your business goals (business energy). No matter which theme you choose to focus on first, ultimately all your activities will help integrate your chakra energy and therefore will benefit all other aspects of yourself, your life, and your business. So, begin where you are and get the rainbow energy flowing. Things will open up energetically in ways you can't imagine!

Putting It Into Practice

It's four-thirty in the afternoon. The RIH fiscal year-end board meeting starts at five o'clock. Megan is working with a client, as are most of the other practitioners at RIH. Those who are not with a client are taking advantage of the new meditation room that is open to team members, clients, and the community at no cost. A local community member volunteers her time weekly to teach meditation techniques to anyone who is interested.

The room is decorated in brown and green earth tones. Soft music plays in the muted light of the floor-to-ceiling salt lamps. Meditation cushions are scattered across the floor. Water from the indoor stone waterfall runs down the far wall into a shallow pool. Valerie and a few other team members sit quietly in meditation on cushions near the waterfall. There are a few clients and community members in the room as well.

After twenty minutes, Valerie stands up and walks down the hall to the boardroom. She smiles and greets team members and clients as she goes. She pauses at the door, registers her energy, acknowledges her fears, then releases her negative energy before entering the room.

The board meeting tonight will focus on goal attainment over the last year. Valerie is nervous. Not all the goals were met, and some have changed, but progress is being made on all. Susan, the board chair, gets down to business and reads off the RIH short-term goals:

- Goal 1 – Financial
  RIH will increase after-tax profits by 10 percent by the end of the current fiscal year.
- Goal 2 – Marketing and Sales
  Launch holistic women's health services by the end of the current fiscal year.
- Goal 3 – Human Resources
  Increase continuing education for all staff to twenty-four hours per person per year by the end of the current fiscal year.
- Goal 4 – Operations
  By the end of the current fiscal year, increase billable hours by 5 percent while improving medical outcomes by 10 percent.
- Goal 5 – Community
  Host community luncheon two times annually by the end of the current fiscal year.

Howard, the CPA and board treasurer, reports that profits did increase over the course of the year, but only by 8 percent rather than the 10 percent budgeted. Valerie feels her face turn hot at this report. The voice of her inner mob breaks her meditative calm. Her inner mob tells her that other team members weren't doing their fair share of the work, and that is why profits are lower. Nine months before, Valerie would have voiced those thoughts, but she has been working with a coach and meditating daily. She now recognizes the voices of false fears. Instead, she tells the board that the team has worked really hard.

Howard continues his report. While the billable hours have increased by 10 percent, it became necessary to hire more practitioners. That and the money spent on the meditation room took a bite out of profits. In the long run, these are great strategic moves, but those decisions reduced RIH's profitability in the short run.

Quality assurance volunteers José and Fatimah report that regulatory compliance is excellent and that client outcomes have improved by a whopping 20 percent. Devon, the board marketing and sales volunteer, further explains that client satisfaction is up 50 percent since the implementation of the mediation room, which may also have something to do with the client outcomes. Valerie adds that the community meditation class has taken the place of the community luncheons previously set as a goal. It is very popular and clients, community, and staff have an opportunity to get to know each other before and after the class.

Lunch and Learn continuing education classes have been replaced by a self-directed personal growth initiative. Progress is discussed at individual strategy sessions twice annually. Additionally, the entire team has been trained in the PeerSpirit Process. Monthly, the team gathers for half a day to discuss and find solutions to some of the more difficult issues. Valerie sheepishly admits the first several months were focused on leadership issues.

Susan asks about the progress on the holistic women's health services. Again, Valerie hears the inner mob chanting "failure" in her head. "Thank God, I meditated before I came," she thinks. She speaks from her heart. "I believe I have found the right holistically minded RN to head up the project. Next, she will be interviewed by the team. The RIH team felt we had more important issues to resolve before bringing in someone new. It took me a while to see the wisdom in that, but I think we all feel ready for that step now."

Overall, the board agrees that positive progress is being made at RIH, albeit slower than expected. Susan praises Valerie for taking the initiative to set the tone for personal growth and open, honest communication. She is particularly pleased with the team approach to problem-solving and the innovative thinking that has brought practitioners, clients, and community together.

Over the last nine months, Valerie has learned that leaders must be willing to be vulnerable and do their personal work in order to be successful. Her work has focused on several chakras. Her constant fear of failure and feelings of not belonging are largely first chakra imbalances. She initially compensated for these imbalances through the use of excessive third chakra power fueled by a great deal of anger lodged in her second chakra.

Because of these imbalances, Valerie's rainbow energy was unable to flow into her upper chakras effectively. She operated mostly from her lower chakras. This left her at a distinct disadvantage as a leader. Now she is learning to lead from her heart wisdom (fourth chakra), communicate authentically (fifth chakra), tap into her business intuition (sixth chakra), and seek help from her Higher Power (seventh chakra).

As Valerie works on her own imbalances and encourages her team to do the same, the organization will benefit greatly, as will their clients and the larger community.

Be the Change

As Gandhi stated, "Be the change you wish to see in the world." Or, in this case, the change you wish to see in your business. As the leader, change begins with you. Sprinkle your energetic stardust throughout your business and share it with your team so they too can become the most they can be. Sharing your gifts and allowing others to share theirs will energetically attract the highest good into your business.

You will always be in the process of becoming. You never really get there. The beauty of this is that you have the potential to become more – more grounded, more empathetic, more empowered, more compassionate, more connected, more intuitive, more spiritual. Never stop becoming! You are an infinite being with infinite potential, and your business is an extension of your magnificence.

Blessings and rainbows on your journey!

Guided Journey: Medicine Bear Woman

On your path to wholeness, you may carry strong negative energy resulting in body pain, illness, or a sickness of the soul. When you are in this state, logic and reason don't help. To move beyond your distress, you must become neutral – you must become a witness, an observer of yourself. You must tap into the power of your inner shaman.

A shaman works with the subtle energies in the universe and will help you transcend the negative energies affecting you. She helps you journey to other worlds by weaving the threads of time and space to bring healing and wholeness. She invites you to create something new – new thoughts, new beliefs, new energetic patterns. As your perceptions change, you shift and step into wholeness. This guided journey is to assist you in doing exactly that.

> *Allow yourself to get in touch with the places in your mind, body, and soul where you feel discomfort, illness, or pain. Imagine your discomfort as a mountain of red sandstone in an arid landscape. The mountain lies in an immense valley filled with low scrub brush, cacti, and dry grasses. Flat-topped, sandstone mountains called mesas encircle the entire valley.*

> *The sun is rising in a cloudless, brilliant-turquoise sky. Take a deep, cleansing breath of the clean, dry air. It seems you are all alone. Yet, as you look around, you realize there are unseen creatures here, creatures that know how to thrive in this arid land – snakes, lizards, rabbits, foxes. They know to drink the dew in the morning from the cacti and to move underground when it is too hot.*

> *Study your mountain a moment. What do you notice about its features? How does it represent your particular discomfort? As you*

contemplate this, you see a narrow trail carved into the side. It is steep and zigzags to some unseen destination.

A sinewy tree with light silver-green leaves obscures the trailhead. In the topmost branch sits the biggest hawk you have ever seen. She looks at you with her intelligent, far-seeing hawk eyes. She seems to be waiting for you. Hawk is known for bringing messages, rebirth, foresight, and a higher vision.

With a loud scree-scree, she flies high into the air, zigzagging her way higher and higher until you lose sight of her. In that moment, you understand that you must follow the zigzag path up the mountain to the very end to find the vision of wholeness you seek. Take a moment to set your intentions before setting out on your journey. As you step onto the trail, Hawk's approval of your decision is clear. She swoops low and celebrates with another loud scree-scree, then disappears in the turquoise blue of the sky.

The trail is narrow and dusty. Each footstep creates a small cloud of fine red sand, and you are soon dusted with the powder. As you walk, the sun moves directly overhead, and you start to feel exceedingly hot. Your feet softly drum on the trail – thump, thump, thump, thump. Slowly you shift to focus solely on the action of hiking. It requires you to dig deep within yourself for resources you didn't know you had.

You continue zigzagging back and forth up the sandstone trail for some time before you pause in the shade beneath a stunted pine tree that, amazingly, clings to the shallow, sandy soil on the mountainside. You begin to see beyond the red sandstone. You notice Jackrabbit nibbling on the dry grass in the shade. And despite the sparse appearance of this landscape, you realize abundance lives here too.

Jackrabbit looks at you intently and then bounds away on his powerful hind legs. He reminds you that within every life there are cycles, and every cycle has its own kind of abundance. Where is the abundance in your business right now? Where do you feel gratitude?

You are approaching a crevice in the mountain, beyond which you cannot see. A few more steps, and you will be there. Already you feel a shift in the air as it becomes cooler and moister. Just before you turn into the crevice, Snake slithers off the trail in front of you where it had been sunning itself. In its place lies a translucent snakeskin.

This is a positive sign. Snake knows it must shed its skin in order to grow, just as you must shed those things no longer working for you. Snake is a symbol of your healing, transformation, and rebirth. What do you need to release in order to rebirth?

You turn into the crevice. The trail continues between two very narrow sandstone walls, yet you see light not far up ahead. You think of Snake and slither through the narrow passage. As you do, you brush against the walls, sending a tingling sensation throughout your body. You have the oddest feeling that you are shedding a layer of unwanted skin just like Snake.

Finally, you step out into the open and are met by a huge sandstone amphitheater. The natural beauty of its womb-like curves overwhelms you. Subtle shades of red, pink, and purple ripple in the sandstone. Here you are protected from the harsh sun and elements, and you breathe a sigh of relief.

It is dark inside the shady womb of the mountain, and it takes a moment for your eyes to adjust to the dimness. Then it registers. There are hundreds of pueblo dwellings wrapped inside. They look like ancient condominiums built high into the walls of the circular cliffs. Immediately, you want to explore them!

You easily walk to what must have been the central meeting grounds for the Pueblo people who lived here centuries ago. There you find a small spring flowing from the rock and into the thirsty ground. You are parched from your long hike and greedily drink from the spring.

As you rise from your drink, you see a desert fox sitting at the foot of a ladder leading to the next level. It quickly scampers up the ladder and disappears. Fox is known for her cunning, awareness, and speed. With her as your guide, you are sure find what you seek.

With some trepidation you follow Fox, but instead of a dwelling, you find yourself standing above a small hole in the ground. It is the entrance to a kiva, a subterranean ceremonial structure used by shamans and the Pueblo people. Fox sits beside the hole, pointing the way into the kiva with her nose.

It is believed that the hole to the kiva is a vortex into other dimensions. You peer into the cool, dark interior. Although you can see nothing, you hear the faint whispers of the ancient Pueblo people encouraging you to enter. Fox waits patiently. She yips once, as if to say, "It's okay."

To enter the kiva, you turn around to start to climb backwards down a ladder made of small tree limbs. As you do, you face Fox. Is she smiling at you? As you descend into the kiva, you feel an otherworldliness flood in. The air smells of wood smoke, and you hear deep, rhythmic drumming. The ladder seems quite long, and it takes some time to reach the smooth sandstone floor.

You turn and glimpse the soft light of the central fire. Then you notice ancient pictures and symbols etched into the soft walls. What messages do you find in these early human communications? In some strange way, they give you the courage to let go and allow transformation and healing.

Slowly you become aware of the presence of others. Sitting in a circle around the fire on the ground are your guides, angels, and ancestors, all here to help you on your path to balance and wholeness. Take note of who is present.

They invite you into the circle to sit with them. Who sits on your left? When you look to your right, you find yourself face-to-face with your inner shaman. What does she look like? She is here to usher you into a new reality of healing and transformation. Your Shaman asks you to listen intently to the rhythmic drumming – boom, boom, boom. Listening to the drumbeat, you enter a state of altered consciousness. Know that you are safe and protected here.

Your head feels heavy. Your inner shaman stands behind you and places her hands on the top of your head. Slowly her hands become heavier. Curious, you tilt your head back and observe as her hands grow dark, coarse hair and long claws. Slowly she transforms into Medicine Bear Woman, who has powerful healing abilities that will help you recover your divine wholeness.

Her huge paws completely cover your skull, and there is a part of you that fears her awesome power, but then you feel her love, strength, and vulnerability. You are deeply moved to receive her gift of healing.

From the earth, you feel a coil of healing energy snaking up through your chakras. It heals at all levels – physical, mental, emotional, spiritual. At the same time, you feel yourself letting go of the things that no longer serve you. Medicine Bear Woman holds the divine space for you to do this deeply spiritual work. What does it feel like to let go and receive this powerful energy?

Time blurs, and you can't tell if it has been minutes, hours, or days since your healing began. Eventually you become aware that the drumming has stopped, and quiet envelops you as you sit before the fire on the smooth ground. You are now alone in the kiva, yet you know that Spirit, your guides, your ancestors, and Medicine Bear Woman live within you.

You stand up and then make your way back to the ladder and climb out of the kiva. A new moon sits in a sky of millions of stars. You easily pick out Ursa Major, the Great Bear constellation. You feel completely whole and one with the universe.

Great Owl lands at your side. She is here to help you realize your new life filled with wisdom, wholeness, and liberation. You find you have no trouble climbing on her back, and you settle into her warm, soft feathers. Feel the cool air rush around you as you rise into the air. Breathe deeply of the night air. As you inhale, your heart chakra expands to receive the infinite energy of the universe. Fully engage with your universal unity.

Higher and higher you fly until you see the whole desert valley bathed in moonlight. You find you are completely open to the moon's energy. Feel her magnetic force touch your third eye chakra and energize your intuitive powers.

Connected to your intuition, you navigate your way to a natural hot mineral spring. You slide gracefully off Great Owl to the ground. As your feet land, you sense a deep connection with the earth, followed by a grounded sense of safety and support.

Completely supported, you disrobe and step into the water for a ritual cleansing. Inhale the rich smell of the minerals as they replenish your body, mind, and spirit. Feel the water's energy cleansing each chakra. Ride the rainbow energy as it courses through you, starting at the root chakra and flowing through your crown chakra. It brings you wholeness, health, and ease.

This energetic openness is your natural state. As you move into the next phase of your soul journey, you innately know how to use your chakra energy for the well-being of your body, life, and business. Maintaining the open energy of your chakras, return your awareness to ordinary reality when you hear the chimes.

❧ **Notes** ❧

Appendix 1
Business Chakra Solutions Guide

While this is not a complete guide to all the business chakra issues that may arise, it covers the most prevalent ones. When working with deficient (D) and excessive (E) chakra energy, it is important to recognize that both of these imbalances are a result of childhood wounding. This wounding causes either avoidance behaviors, which create deficient energy (D) in a chakra, or overcompensating behaviors, which create excessive energy (E) in a chakra. A wounding may even cause both avoidance and overcompensating behaviors, and thereby both deficient and excessive energy (D/E) in the same chakra.

If you are uncertain whether a particular issue in your business chakra falls under D or E, sit with the question for a while. See if you can feel in your own body what the answer might be. It's quite possible that you may experience an issue listed as D in the guide to be more E, or an issue classified as E to actually be more D. You even may experience an issue as a bit of both D and E. Use your own inner guidance; you are your own best resource for this. Even if you aren't sure what the exact nature of the chakra imbalance is (D or E), don't despair! Your chakra will still return to balance when you work with it.

Happy chakra balancing!

BUSINESS CHAKRA SOLUTIONS GUIDE

Category	Issue or Obstacle	Chakra(s)	Deficient (D) Excessive (E)	Chapter(s)
Communication	Biases	5	D/E	7
	Body language – reading	5	D	7
	Conflict	5	E	7
	Difficulties	2, 5	D/E	4, 7
	Disagreements	5	E	7
	Dishonesty	5	D/E	7
	Distortions	5	E	7
	Hard conversations	5	D/E	7
	Inauthentic	5	D/E	7
	Listening – poor	5	D/E	7
	Meetings – unproductive	5	D/E	7
	Nonverbal cues	5	D	7
	Personalities – difficult	5	E	7
	Speaking skills – poor	5	D/E	7
	Style – uncertain	5	D	7
	Truth – speaking	5	D	7
Core Values	Core values – none/unclear	3	D/E	5
	Ethics/ideals – poor	3, 7	D	5, 9

	Ethics/ideals – undefined	3, 7	D	5, 9
	Goals – not related	3	D	5
	Purpose – undefined	3, 7	D	3, 9
Creativity	Change – poor response	2	D	4
	Curiosity killed	5	D	7
	Imagination – lack of	2, 6	D	4, 8
	Implementation – poor	3	D/E	5
	Inflexible	2, 6	D	4, 8
	Innovation – poor/none	2, 6	D	4, 6
	Mistakes – fear of	2, 4	E	4, 6
	Professional growth – lacking	2, 4, 7	D	4, 6, 9
	Problem-solving – poor	4, 6	D	6, 8
Culture	Belonging – lack of	1, 5	D	3, 7
	Counterculture behavior	5	D/E	7
	Energy – bad vibe	2	D/E	4
	Health practices – poor	1	D/E	3
	Negative	4, 5	D	6, 7

	Team respect – poor	3	E	5
	Work hours – too long	1, 3	E	3, 5
	Work pleasure – lack of	2	D	4
Customers	Attracting ideal – ability	4, 7	D	6, 9
	Communication – poor	5	D/E	7
	Customer service – poor	2, 5	D	4, 7
	Dissatisfied	2, 3, 4, 5	D	4, 5, 6, 7
	Ideal – undefined	4, 5	D	6, 7
Decisions	Difficult	3, 4, 6	D	5, 6, 8
	Fear of	6, 7	D/E	8, 9
	Indecisive	3, 4, 6	D/E	5, 6, 8
	Poor outcomes	3, 4, 6	D/E	5, 6, 8
	Repetitive	4, 6	D	6, 8
	Unbalanced	3, 4, 6	E	5, 6, 8
	Uncentered	4, 6	D	6, 8
	Uncertain	3, 4, 6	D/E	5, 6, 8
Emotions	Disconnected	2	D	4
	Drama/mood rules the day	2	E	4
	Energetic effect	2	D/E	4
	Fear	1, 2	D/E	3, 4

	Feelings underground	2	D/E	4
	Negative	2	D/E	4
	Productivity – poor	2	D/E	4
	Unresolved	2	D/E	4
Financial	Cash flow – poor	1, 4	D	3, 6
	Cash reserves – low	1, 4	E	3, 6
	Debt – high	1, 4	E	3, 6
	Fear	1, 2, 4	E	3, 4, 6
	Giving back – none	4	D	6
	Profitability – poor	1, 4	D	3, 6
	Scarcity thinking	1, 4	D/E	3, 6
	Sustainability	1	D/E	3
	Wage/benefits – poor	1, 4	D	3, 6
Goals	Challenging	3, 6	E	5, 8
	Difficulty making	3, 4	D/E	5, 6
	Faith in goals – poor	7	D	9
	Focus – lack of	3	E	5
	Goals – none/ unclear	3	D	5
	Intentions – lack of	3, 6	D	5, 8

	Manifesting – fall short	3, 4, 7	D/E	5, 6, 9
	Too many	3	E	5
Intuition	Business instincts – poor	6	D	8
	Challenges	4, 6	D/E	6, 8
	Communication – poor	5, 6	D/E	7, 8
	Direction – lack of	6	D/E	8
	Disconnection	6	D/E	8
	Distrust of	6	D/E	8
	Fear of future/ unknown	6	D/E	8
	Imagination – lack of	6	D	8
	Intentions – none	4, 6	D/E	6, 8
	Solutions – few	2, 4, 6	D	4, 6, 8
Leadership	Clear direction – lack of	4, 6	D/E	6, 8
	Controlling	3	E	5
	Courage – lack of	4	D	6
	Ethics - poor	7	D/E	9
	Heart centeredness – lack of	4	D	6
	Inspiration – lack of	2, 3	D/E	4, 5

	Judgment – poor	4	E	6
	Leadership – negative	7	D/E	9
	Meetings – unproductive	5	D/E	7
	Respect – poor	3	D/E	5
	Soul path – unknown	2, 4, 5	D	4, 6, 7
	Spiritual connection – poor	7	D	9
	Support of others – poor	2	D/E	4
	Thoughts – negative	7	D	9
Marketing	Authenticity – lacking	5	D/E	7
	Customers – too few	5	D	7
	Customers – undefined	3, 5	D	5, 7
	Ethics – poor	5	D	7
	Focus – none/ poor	5	D/E	7
	Manifesting destiny – ability	4, 5	D	6, 7
	Message – poor/ unclear	5	D/E	7
	Passion – lack of	2	D	4
	SWOT – lack of	5	D/E	7
	Values – poor/ unclear	3, 5	D/E	5, 7

Mission	Faith in business – lack	7	D	9
	Ideal customer – undefined	2	D	4
	Mission – none/ unclear	2, 4	D/E	4, 6
	Passion – none/ poor	2	D	4
	Purpose – none/ poor	2	D	4
	Walk the talk – poor	3, 5	D/E	5, 7
Motivation	Celebrations – few	2, 4	D/E	4, 6
	Interest – lack of	2	D	4
	Mistakes – punished	2	E	4
	Motivation – lack of	2	D	4
	Negativity	2	D/E	4
	Passion – lack of	2	D	4
	Productivity – poor	2	D/E	4
	Workaholism	3, 4	D/E	5, 6
Power	Authority – too little	3	D	5
	Authority – too much	3	E	5
	Competitive – overly	3	E	5

	Competitive – ability	3	D	5
	Disempowerment	3	D/E	5
	Expansion – lack of	1, 7	D	3, 9
	Expansion – only focus	1, 3	E	3, 5
	Fear as motivation	1, 2, 3	E	3, 4, 5
	Imbalance	3	D/E	5
	Power – overbearing	3	E	5
	Shared decision-making – poor/ none	3	E	5
Relationships	Communication – poor	5	D/E	7
	Conflict – high	2	E	4
	Disconnected	2	D	4
	Dishonest	2	E	4
	Give & take – imbalance	2, 4	D/E	4, 6
	Unresolved	2	D/E	4
	Unstable	2	D/E	4
Structure	Environment sustainability – poor	1	D/E	3
	Insurance – none/poor	1	D	3

	Legal entity – not ideal	1	D/E	3
	Lines of authority – unclear	1	D	3
	Major change occurring	1	E	3
	Organizational chart – none or unclear	1	D/E	3
	Unstable climate	1	E	3
	Work roles – undefined	1	E	3
Success	Failure	1, 7	E	3, 9
	Mindset – poor	1, 7	D	3, 9
Synchronicity	Power of attraction	2, 4	D	4, 6
Systems	Job descriptions – poor or none	1	D/E	3
	Policies & procedures – poor or none	1	D/E	3
	Regulatory compliance – poor	1	D/E	3
	Risk management – poor or none	1	D	3
	Systems – poor or none: accounting, inventory, information base, technology, etc.	1	D/E	3

	Time management – poor	7	E	9
	Work flow – poor	1	E	3
Team	Attracting quality	4, 7	D/E	6, 9
	Attitudes – poor	2, 3, 4	D/E	4, 5, 6
	Belonging – poor	1, 5	D	3
	Challenging	4, 5	D/E	6, 7
	Communication – poor	5	D/E	7
	Counter-productive work behaviors	2, 4	D/E	4, 6
	Happiness – lack of	2, 4	D	4, 6
	Job satisfaction – lack of	2, 4	D	4, 6
	Relationships – conflict	2, 4	D/E	4, 6
	Relationships – disconnected	2, 4	D/E	4, 6
	Leadership – none	4, 5	D	6, 7
	Team-building – none	2	D	4
	Team value – lack of	4, 6	D	6, 8
Vision	Focus – poor	2, 3	D/E	4, 5
	Desires – unknown	2, 4	D	4, 6

	Passion – unknown	2	D	4
	Vision statement – none or unclear	2, 4	D/E	4, 6
	Your "why" – unknown	2	D/E	4
Work Environment	Equipment – lack of	1	D	3
	Equipment – poor	1	D	3
	Clutter	7	E	9
	Safety – poor	1	D/E	3
	Workspace – inadequate	1	D	3
	Workspace – too big	1	E	3
	Workspace – uninviting	1, 6	D	3, 8

Appendix 2
Goal Tracking Form

Write down your goal, the start date, and the likely completion date. Next write down the action steps to accomplish the goal and the due date for each step. Check them off when done and record the date completed. Fill out a separate tracking form for each goal.

Goal Tracking Form			
Goal			
Start Date	**Completion Date**		
Due Date	**Action Steps**	**Done**	**Date**

❧ Bibliography ❧

Aroma Tools. *Modern Essentials*. Pleasant Grove, UT: Aroma Tools. 2016. Eighth Edition.

Ask Your Pendulum. *How to Use a Pendulum*. AskYourPendulum.com. Retrieved August 5, 2017.

Assaraf, John and Smith, Murray. *The Answer*. New York: Atria Books. 2008. First Edition.

Baldwin, Christina and Linnea, Ann. *The Circle Way: A Leader in Every Chair*. San Francisco, CA: Berrett-Koehler Publishers, Inc. 2010. First Edition.

Baron-Reid, Colette. *Wealth Energetix Manual*. Hampton, NH: Colette Baron-Reid, Inc., To Amaze, Inc., and Master Intuitive Coaches Institute. 2012. First Edition.

Baron-Reid, Colette. *Weight Release Energetix Manual*. Hampton, NH: Colette Baron-Reid, Inc., To Amaze, Inc., and Master Intuitive Coaches Institute. 2012. First Edition.

Baer, Drake. *How Patagonia's New CEO is Increasing Profits While Trying to Save the World*. New York: Fast Company. 2014.

Blake, Trevor. *Three Simple Steps. A Map to Success in Business and Life*. Dallas TX: BenBella Books, Inc., 2012. First Edition.

Bloch, Douglas and George, Demetra. *Astrology For Yourself*. Oakland, CA: Wingbow Press. 1987. Seventh Edition.

Brown, Brené. *Braving the Wilderness: The Quest for True Belonging and the Courage to Stand Alone*. New York: Random House, LLC. 2017. First Edition.

Byrne, Rhonda. *The Secret*. New York: Atria Books. Hillsboro, 2006. First Edition.

Capra, Fritjof. *The Turning Point*. New York: Bantam Books. 1982. Sixth Edition.

Charman, Rachelle. *Chakra Reading Cards Guidebook*. Summer Hill, NSW: Rockpool Publishing. 2016. First Edition.

Childre, Doc and McCraty, Rollin. *Psychophysiological Correlates of Spiritual Experience*. Boulder Creek, CA: AAPB. 2002.

Choquette, Sonya. *Chakra Remedy Guide: Your Guide for True Balance*. Niles, IL.

Church, Dawson. *EFT for Weight Loss*. Fulton, CA: Energy Psychology Press. 2010. First Edition.

Cirlot, J.E. *A Dictionary of Symbols*. New York: Philosophical Library, Inc. 1971. Second Edition.

Cooper, J.C., *An Illustrated Encyclopeadia of Traditional Symbols*. London, England: Thames and Hudson, Ltd. 1978. Second Edition.

Dale, Cyndi. *The Complete Book of Chakra Healing*. Woodbury, MN: Llewellyn Publications. 2010. Second Edition.

Dillard, Sherrie. *Discover Your Psychic Type*. Woodbury, MN: Llewellyn Publications. 2008. First Edition.

Dispenza, Joe. *You Are the Placebo, Making Your Mind Matter*. Carlsbad, CA: Hay House, Inc. 2014. First Edition.

Drucker, Peter. *Management*. New York: HarperCollins Publishers. 2008. Second Edition.

Eden, Donna and Feinstein, David. *Eden Energy Medicine*; New York: Penguin Group. 2008. First Edition.

Eiker, Diane and Sapphire. *Keep Simple Ceremonies: The Feminist Spiritual Community of Portland, Maine*. Portland, ME: Astarte Shell Press. 1995. First Edition.

Enlighten. *Emotions & Essential Oils*. American Fork, UT: Enlighten Alternative Healing, LLC. 2016. Fifth Edition.

Fontana, David. *The Secret Language of Dreams*. London: Duncan, Baird Publishers. 1994. First Edition.

Godwin, Malcom. *The Lucid Dreamer*. New York: Simon & Schuster. 1994. First Edition.

Grout, Pamela. *E Squared*. Carlsbad, CA: Hay House, Inc. 2013. First Edition.

Hawkins, David. *Letting Go: The Pathway of Surrender*. Carlsbad, CA: Hay House, Inc. 2012. First Edition.

Harvey, Jerry B. *The Abilene Paradox: The Management of Agreement*. Landham, MD: Lexington Books. 1988.

Hiam, Alexander. *Marketing for Dummies*. Hoboken, NJ: Wiley Publishing, Inc. 2009. Third Edition.

Hoffherr, Glen D. and Reid, Robert P., Jr. *The Creativity Toolkit*; New York: McGraw-Hill Companies, Inc. 1999. First Edition.

Horan, Jim. *The One Page Business Plan*. Berkeley, CA: The One Page Business Plan Company. 1997-2011. First Edition.

Isaacs, Nora. *"Is a Kundalini Awakening Safe?"* https://www.yogajournal.com/yoga-101/safe-awaken-snake. Yoga Journal. Boulder, CO: Cruz Bay Publishing, Inc. 2017

Jung, C.G. *Dreams*. Princeton, NJ: Princeton University Press. 1974. Ninth Edition.

Jung, C.G. *Memories, Dreams, Reflections*. New York: Random House. 1963. Third Edition.

Kaufer, Nelly, and Osmer-Newhouse, Carol. *A Woman's Guide to Spiritual Renewal*. New York: HarperCollins Publishers. 1994. First Edition.

Kripner, Stanley. *Dreams and the Development of a Personal Mythology*. Journal of Mind and Behavior. 7, no. 2/3 449-461. 1986.

Lee, Jennifer, *Right Brain Business Plan*. Novato, CA: New World Library, Jennifer Lee. 2011. First Edition.

McCants, Glynis, *Glynis Has Your Number*. San Marino, CA. The Numbers Lady, Inc. 2005. First Edition.

McCraty, Rollin. *Bioelectromagnetic Interactions Within and Between*. Boulder Creek, CA: Heart Math Institute. 2003. https://www.researchgate.net/publication/274451622_The_Energetic_Heart_Biolectromagnetic_Interactions_Within_and_Between_People

McCraty, Rollin. *Science of The Heart*- https://www.researchgate.net/profile/Rollin_Mccraty2/publication/293944391_Science_of_the_Heart_Volume_2_Exploring_the_Role_of_the_Heart_in_Human_Performance_An_Overview_of_Research_Conducted_by_the_HeartMath_Institute/links/56bcf14a08ae6cc737c6adc4/Science-of-the-Heart-Volume-2-Exploring-the-Role-of-the-Heart-in-Human-Performance-An-Overview-of-Research-Conducted-by-the-HeartMath-Institute.pdf Boulder Creek, CA: Heart Math Institute. 2015. First Edition.

McKeown, Greg. *Essentialism: The Disciplined Pursuit of Less*. New York: Random House, LLC. 2014. First Edition.

Mind Tools. *The Mind Tools E-Book, Part II: Personal Productivity and*

Development Tools. Mind Tools, Ltd. 2009. Sixth Edition.

Naparstek, Belleruth. *Your Sixth Sense.* San Francisco: HarperCollins Publishers, Inc. 1997. First Edition.

Pierce, Penny. *The Intuitive Way.* New York: MJF Books. 1997. First Edition.

Pink, Daniel. *A Whole New Mind.* New York: Penguin Group. 2005. First Edition.

Rob. *Patagonia: Aligning Values and Workforce.* https://inafutureage. wordpress.com/2010/10/21/patagonia-aligning-values-and-workforce/ InAFutureAgeWordPresss.com. 2010.

Robbins, Stephen P. and Judge, Timothy A. *Managing Organizational Behaviors.* New York: Pearson Education, Inc. 2017. Seventeenth Edition.

Suazo, Sarah, Baca, Justin and Sawayda, Jennifer, under the direction of Ferrell, O.C. and Ferrell, Linda. *Patagonia: A Sustainable Outlook on Business.* https://danielsethics.mgt.unm.edu/pdf/patagonia.pdf Albuquerque, NM: University of New Mexico. 2012.

Scott, Susan, *Fierce Conversations.* New York: Berkeley Publishing Group. 2004. Second Edition.

Sentier, Elen. *The Celtic Chakras.* Winchester, UK: Moon Books. 2013. First Edition.

Stein, Diane. *The Women's Book of Healing.* New York: Crown Publishing Group. 2004. Second Edition.

Twist, Lynne. *The Soul of Money.* New York: W.W. Norton & Company, Inc. 2003. First Edition.

Worrall, Simon. *How 40,000 Tons of Cosmic Dust Falling to Earth Affects You and Me.* https://news.nationalgeographic.com/2015/01/150128-big-bang-universe-supernova-astrophysics-health-space-ngbooktalk/ Washington, DC: National Geographic. January 28, 2015.

~ Royalty-Free Music ~
Attributions for Guided Journeys

Getting Rooted: *Clean Soul – Calming* by Kevin MacLeod is licensed under a Creative Commons Attribution license. https://creativecommons.org/licenses/by/4.0

Sacred Spring: *Fluidscape* by Kevin MacLeod is licensed under a Creative Commons Attribution license. https://creativecommons.org/licenses/by/4.0/

Power of the Lioness: *White Lotus* by Kevin MacLeod is licensed under a Creative Commons Attribution license. http://creativecommons.org/licenses/by/3.0/

The Heart of Quan Yin: *Wisps of Whorls* by Kevin MacLeod is licensed under a Creative Commons Attribution license. http://creativecommons.org/licenses/by/3.0/

Play Your Music: *Angel's Dream* by Aakash Gandhi is available from YouTube's free Audio Library.

Moon Pool: *Avec Soin - Romance* by Kevin MacLeod is licensed under a Creative Commons Attribution license. https://creativecommons.org/licenses/by/4.0/

Wise Sage: *Light Awash* by Kevin MacLeod is licensed under a Creative Commons Attribution license. https://creativecommons.org/licenses/by/4.0/)

Medicine Bear Woman: *Isolated* by Kevin MacLeod is licensed under a Creative Commons Attribution license. https://creativecommons.org/licenses/by/4.0/

❦ *About the Author* ❦

Melissa J. Albert Photography

As an executive coach, entrepreneur, author, teacher, artist, energy healer, intuitive, and essential oils advocate, Nanette Giacoma walks between the worlds of traditional and alternative business practices. Integrating 25-plus years of business experience and 11 years of coaching experience with unconventional methods, Nanette works holistically with her clients to help them achieve the kind of professional and personal success they desire. She lives for those profound moments of insight that are the harbingers of change and transformation, both for her clients and herself. Nanette has an MBA and an MA in Art and Consciousness Studies, and she is a Usui and Kundalini Reiki Master. Nanette is also a Certified Master Intuitive Coach from Colette Baron-Reid's Master Intuitive Coaches Institute.

A cowgirl at heart, Nanette's roots are in Park City, Utah. She lived in eight different states, including several major cities, before finding her forever home in Maine, where she has resided for the last 19 years. Nanette lives there with her husband, daughter, and a menagerie of large and small animals, including horses. On any given morning (even in winter), you will find her walking with her dog down to the river to meditate before work.

Contact Information

- For the downloadable forms and recordings of the guided journeys mentioned in the book, please go to Nanette's website at http://nanettegiacoma.com/OpenForBusinessBook.

- A complete description of the services Nanette offers as well as her latest schedule of workshops and speaking events can also be found at http://nanettegiacoma.com.

- Nanette welcomes inquiries and contact from readers and can be reached via email at Nanette@nanettegiacoma.com

(continued ~Reviews)

Nanette Giacoma is a masterful writer and has integrated an immense expanse of knowledge into this book. Nanette is especially gifted because she is bilingual. She speaks the language of business with her MBA and corporate experience. She also speaks the language of spirit and energy and merges them into the most beautiful images representing the chakras.

She has woven together a certain wisdom and has the courage to voice it, sharing the energy of the divine feminine. Her writing opens up new possibilities for women in business, helping to transform the way we do our work by tapping into our source of knowing and the universal life energy we all seek.

As a doctor, I know the ways blockages can manifest in the body; like thyroid disease when we don't speak our truth, and the throat chakra becomes blocked. As a business owner, I know how energy blockages can undermine the function of our work causing us to feel stuck, making the same mistakes over and over. Open for Business offers amazing guidance for every woman who has an interest in her body and soul being balanced with work.

Nanette has helped guide me in unravelling the hidden messages I was raised with and connect to a spirit guide who helps direct my decisions. I look forward to using this book to do chakra clearing to further strengthen the success of my practice, and aid in my own personal transformation.

Sarah Ackerly, *Naturopathic Doctor*
Northern Sun Family Healthcare and Birth Center
www.northernsunfamilyhealthcare.com

i Rob. *Patagonia: Aligning Values and Workforce.* InAFutureAgeWordPresss.com. 2010.

ii Manifestation Board adapted from the vision board process by CEO of Body Mind Health. (van Zandbergen and Washburn n.d.)

iii Hertzing, Bill. *What's at the Core of Rackspace Core Values?* San Antonio, TX: Rackspace Blog. 2016.

iv http://financials.morningstar.com/direct/ratios/r.html?t=XETR:R42&region=deu&culture=en-US&productcode=MLE&cur=. Morning Star Financials 2015.

v Adapted from *"Putting Down the Stones"*; a guided meditation by Elker, Diane, and Sapphire. *Keep Simple Ceremonies: The Feminist Spiritual Community of Portland, Maine.* Portland, ME: Astarte Shell Press. 1995. First Edition.

vi Sentier, Elen. A Spiral path is adapted from *Journey: the Spiral Path* in Elen Sentier's book *The Celtic Chakras.* Moon Books/John Hunt Publishing, UK. 2013.

CPSIA information can be obtained
at www.ICGtesting.com
Printed in the USA
FSHW022310071218
54224FS

9 781732 916906